The Middle
Management
Challenge

The Middle Management Challenge

Moving from Crisis to Empowerment

Alan L. Frohman
Frohman Associates

Leonard W. Johnson
Boston University

*Barry —
your ideas
were the original
spark that got me
started on the middles!
with many thanks,
Leonard
January 1993*

see p. 26, 30, 40

McGraw-Hill, Inc.
New York St. Louis San Francisco Auckland Bogotá
Caracas Lisbon London Madrid Mexico Milan
Montreal New Delhi Paris San Juan São Paulo
Singapore Sydney Tokyo Toronto

Library of Congress Cataloging-in-Publication Data

Frohman, Alan L., date.
   The middle management challenge : moving from crisis to
empowerment / Alan L. Frohman, Leonard W. Johnson.
      p.   cm.
  Includes index.
  ISBN 0-07-022512-5:
   1. Middle managers—United States. 2. Industrial management—
United States. 3. Competition—United States. I. Johnson,
Leonard W., date. II. Title.
HD38.25.U6F76 1992
658.4′3—dc20   92-24876
                                                   CIP

1 2 3 4 5 6 7 8 9 0 DOC/DOC 9 8 7 6 5 4 3 2

ISBN 0-07-022512-5

*The sponsoring editor for this book was Karen Hansen, the editing supervisor
was Fred Dahl, and the production supervisor was Suzanne W. Babeuf. It was
set in Baskerville by Inkwell Publishing Services.*

Printed and bound by R. R. Donnelley & Sons Company.

This book is printed on recycled, acid-free paper containing a minimum of 50% recycled de-
inked fiber.

We dedicate this book to our fathers,
Edgar Frohman and John Johnson,
who showed us that there are great opportunities
for all who try to accomplish things.

Contents

Preface

Why We Wrote This Book

We believe that people in the middle levels of most organizations have very difficult jobs. What makes their positions almost impossible is that the real nature of their jobs is unrecognized—that they must deal with inconsistent signals and changing messages. Coupled with a feeling of powerlessness, these elements make the jobs of middle managers full of frustration, disappointment, and anger that ultimately result in a death of spirit.

The focus on leaders does not go far enough. Leaders can produce visions and strategies, align resources, build networks, and so on. Yet, if they are not willing to remove the chains on those in the middle levels, their visions and strategies will founder. It is time to understand that U.S. industry has two principal problems: insufficient leadership and walled-off, turned-off middle managers. This book addresses the second problem.

We are not pessimistic about this situation. Look at what has been accomplished, even with the middle levels so hamstrung! Just as a start, we feel a great deal can be accomplished by understanding what needs to be done to unleash the potential of middle managers. We are continually amazed at the strength, courage, and initiative taken by middle managers once they perceive an opportunity.

We must start looking at the people in the middle as part of the solution to what plagues American industry, not just as part of the problem. We don't mean lip service. Management must take action to introduce new structures and practices to build a more "horizontal" organization. The reasons that this process must be undertaken and how to do it are discussed in this book.

We are writing for all managers, in large or small organizations, manufacturing or service, public or private, for-profit or not-for-profit. The topics we address are not a function of size, balance sheet, or ownership. They are a function of a hierarchical structure and an environment of change and uncertainty—conditions virtually all organizations face today.

Who is a middle manager? We find that there is a good deal of confusion on this point. There is no universally applicable definition because the people performing the functions of middle management vary widely from organization to organization. We find that it is most useful to define the term "middle manager" broadly, that is, beginning at first-level supervisor and ending just below the level of executives who have company-wide responsibilities.

How the Book Is Organized

We begin with a Prologue introducing EMI,[1] a large manufacturing company confronted with a list of the challenges and problems faced by many U.S. companies. We revisit EMI again in Chap. 7 to discuss the actions EMI took to address their challenges. Finally, in the Epilogue we return two years later to assess the results of these actions for the people at EMI and on the company's bottom line.

In Part 1, we describe why we believe that it is counterproductive to think of middle managers as the scapegoats for the loss of American competitiveness. The merge, purge, and leverage mania of the 1980s is not the long-term answer. Rather, in the 1990s, a world-class competitor must establish the capacity to keep pace with technology, anticipate market changes, introduce innovative products, meet exacting quality standards, and manage the complexities of being a truly global firm. We must think of middle managers not as obstacles but as the source of the capabilities that are essential to compete effectively in this environment.

By the mid-1980s, our work as consultants led us to suspect that there was a "gap" at the middle-manager level in many organizations. However, our review of traditional thinking on this subject, which is described in Chap. 2, indicated that other people had not found evidence of such a gap. Thinking that this traditional view might be out of date, we decided to conduct a study of our own as a basis for assessing whether, in fact, life for middle managers had changed in the 1980s.

From the results of our study, which are described in Chap. 3, we concluded that the gap in the middle is real. In fact, we found the gap across a wider range of business and organizational issues than we had expected. We also concluded that the gap results from a critical lack of information sharing, cooperation, and teamwork—which are especially important for middle managers to be effective in their jobs.

In Part 2, we begin by showing what it is like taking the heat in the middle of a traditional, hierarchical organization. Organizations have always had a vertical, or up-down structure. Today, vertical systems are overloaded and the up-down channels are clogged. As a result, we find that many middle managers feel out of touch and isolated behind the walls of their own departments. Even worse, they now find that they lack the broad experience and perspective essential for further promotion. For many middle managers, the merge and purge syndrome and delayering have had the effect of "dead ending" their careers.

Turning the corner in Chap. 5, we describe a very different organization where there is a balance between the vertical and lateral dimensions. In the "balanced organization," the walls are knocked down and middle managers are more able to provide the resources needed for their firms to compete. With the addition of lateral structures and procedures, the vertical channels carry less of the "traffic." The relationship with the boss and with subordinates changes, and middle managers are treated more like partners.

In Part 3, we turn our attention from description to prescription. Our focus is on the specific action steps that senior and middle managers need to take to knock down the walls and unleash the potential. The old view of top management and management structure won't work if the potential from the middle is to be realized. Supplementing the top-down structure is a lateral structure that requires a new role for top management. Senior managers need to challenge their traditional assumptions about organization and control. They must also reevaluate their long-held beliefs about focusing on short-term results, managing middle managers, competition between departments, and who should initiate actions.

In an organization where there is leadership from the middle, what is considered successful job performance changes dramatically. The Peter Principle is dead! Instead, the emphasis is on promoting risk taking, taking action, and accepting mistakes in small doses. In Chap. 7, we return to EMI to see what actions they took to close the gap in the middle and respond to the challenges facing them.

In this process, the job of middle managers does not become any easier. Instead, their work is even more demanding as they are now initiating action, not reacting to events. The psychological challenges are greater, but so are the opportunities to make a difference. We conclude Part 3 with a discussion of what middle managers can do to prepare for taking charge in the middle.

In summary, then, in the first half of the book we look at why middle managers are important and why there is a gap in the middle. In the second half, we turn our attention to actions that senior and middle managers can take to realize the potential of this group that is so essential if we are to meet the challenges of today's competitive reality.

Acknowledgments

We would like to acknowledge the contributions of a number of our clients to this book. They include Jack Smith, Lloyd Reuss, Don Pais, Dick Donnelly, and Bob Jones at General Motors; Eric Mittelstadt at GMFanuc Robotics; John Bush at Gillette; John Balboni and Dick Lacana at Veratec (a division of International Paper); John Buono at Analytical Answers, Inc., Chuck Kolb at Aerodyne; and Bill Wright of Wright Associates.

We would also like to recognize the professional guidance and support we received from our brothers, Mark Frohman and Keith Johnson. We also owe a considerable intellectual debt to our colleagues at the Boston University School of Management: Lloyd Baird, Dave Brown, and Tim Hall.

Finally, we appreciate the patience, encouragement, and guidance provided by our editor, Karen Hansen, at McGraw-Hill.

Alan L. Frohman
Leonard W. Johnson

Endnote

1. EMI and several other company names used in this book are not the actual names of the companies, but the situations described are real.

Prologue: The New Competitive Reality at EMI

David Frank, president of EMI, was very frustrated. It was the winter of 1988, and for the last several decades his organization had been a world leader in the production of electric motors. But this leadership seemed to be slipping away. It was not for a lack of good ideas, good technology, or good products. He saw it slipping because of a lack of ability within his organization to act on and successfully implement new ideas.

There are many examples he cited to us, the consultants he had brought in to help him deal with the problem. The first example he cited was a joint venture with a Chinese company that promised to be very positive for both companies as well as for the two countries involved. But he had no one outside of himself to work on the joint venture. He was too busy to pound out the details and see it through to implementation. As a result, the joint venture went nowhere. He also described a history of new-product ideas that, whether they came from his sales organization or R&D organization, took too much time to move into the marketplace. Finally, he worried that below his vice presidents, there was a lack of depth of management talent.

Making matters worse was a future of competition even more fierce than the past and present. Foreign competition was coming into his market, and Japanese companies, in particular, were coming over with competitive products at better prices. David's real concern was competitors' ability to bring new technology into the marketplace a lot faster than he was able to. He realized it would not be long before they were introducing products that were *superior* in performance faster than he could.

He was very proud of his organization and its people. They had been leaders in their field for decades, but he felt there was something wrong now. He wanted to find out what it was. He asked us, as consultants, to look at his organization and to help identify what he could do to turn the organization around.

We interviewed a cross-section of employees at all levels. The answers were fairly consistent and one quote will be used to summarize what we found: "We have hot shots on top, new energetic employees on the bottom, and plateaued, average performers in the middle." People were telling us that the gap in the middle, the walling off of middle managers, was a serious problem. Good people were being brought in, and the best made it to the top. But the middle of the organization was being suffocated and walled off, and was underperforming as a result. The following five categories summarize the other findings from the interviews.

Performance Must Dramatically Increase

The first finding was that performance, quality, and productivity rates would have to increase dramatically, accompanied by major shifts in skills and resources to achieve their five-year goals. Figures P.1 and P.2 identify the kinds of changes that needed to occur over the next five years in order to perform up to the level stated in the business plan. At the same time, the business plan called for increased productivity, as shown in Fig. P.3. The requirements for increased efficiency meant that headcount over the next five years would have to be held stable or decline. The organization faced a tremendous challenge to meet the goals set forth in its business plans for the next five years. But, in light of its competitive reality, it had no choice.

Good People Were Being Hired

EMI was, in fact, hiring very good people. The new hires were seen by their colleges as being the best in the class. EMI's reputation on campus was very good, so that it had little difficulty attracting high-caliber stu-

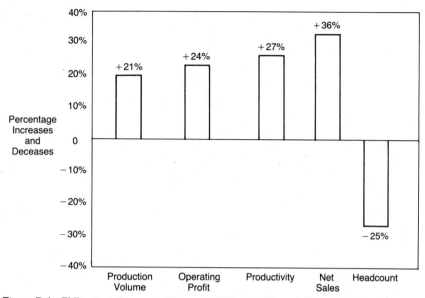

Figure P.1. EMI projected increases/decreases, 1988–1993 (from the EMI 1988–1993 Business Plan). Over a five-year period, EMI is projected to increase its production volume 21%, operating profit 25%, productivity 27%, net sales 36%, and decrease its headcount 25%.

dents. The company also hired from some of the best schools. Our discussions with some of the new recruits indicated a lot of excitement and enthusiasm for their new employer. They had joined the company because of the expected challenge and opportunities. It was clear that turned-on, good people were being attracted to join. It was something that was happening after they joined that began turning them off. We also found that the turnover was relatively low and that the people who stayed in the organization tended to be the good performers they wanted to retain. Good people were being hired and kept; clearly something was affecting their performance other than ability.

Human-Resource Management Systems Not Helping

We found that the human-resource management systems that were in place were not really helping the people in the organization to grow and develop. High-potential people who were identified tended to be kept by their bosses in their functional area. One employee told us:

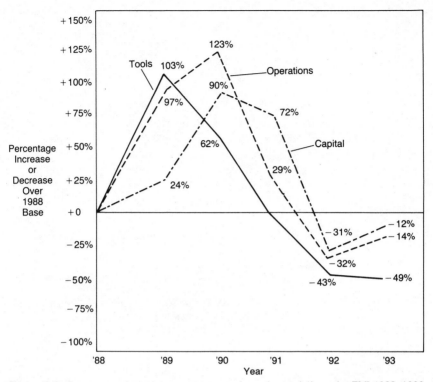

Figure P.2. Investment changes in operations, tools, and capital (from the EMI 1988–1993 Busines Plan). Major investments in operations, tools, and capital will require major shifts in skills and resources.

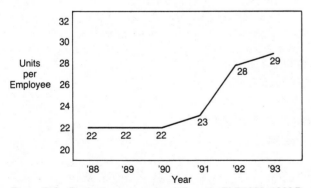

Figure P.3. Production per employee (from the EMI 1988–1993 Business Plan). Production per employee must jump up dramatically.

High-potential managers are left to live and die in their own functions. There is no mechanism in place to see that high-potential people are doing their best for the company.

A rotation program was little used. A middle manager commented:

I should have been rotated to other jobs long ago. Experiences that I should have had in other functions have been lost. Opportunities for me to contribute were lost.

We need to move people earlier in their careers, and more frequently. We are used to operating only as a functional organization. It is very difficult now to link across boundaries.

Performance appraisals tended to be focused on specific, technically oriented goals. The training programs tended to emphasize primarily functional skills (e.g., accounting) more than they did management or team-building skills. Manpower planning and career planning tended to be confined within functional units and were used or not used depending on the predilection of the functional managers. In the words of an employee:

We have the people. They are good and energetic people. But we don't establish the paths for them to work with their peers in another part of the organization. The only path available to a person is for him to talk to his manager.

Out of 146 individuals in positions in upper middle management, we could identify only 14 who had cross-functional experience within the last 10 years. The average manager's career was fully within his functional unit. The employees saw these factors as limiting their capacity to perform.

Lateral Communication Difficult

Lateral communication—communication across functional boundaries—was encouraged much less than needed. Some of the quotes from the middle managers that support this finding are reported below.

Communicating across functional boundaries isn't rejected, it's just that when you try to talk to somebody in another part of the organization, it's like shouting into a bottomless pit.

I was never told I needed to communicate effectively with my peers in other parts of the organization. When I did it and a project was better for it, it never appeared on my evaluation.

> We don't reward people who attempt to work collaboratively with other parts of the organization. But we do execute people for failing to get their job done.

> There is no room or time for trying to work collaboratively or helping people in other parts of the organization.

> I had the impression that keeping my mouth shut when talking to other parts of the organization was desired.

> We have a bureaucracy of checks and balances here rather than a team that works together to solve problems.

> If I try to work with people in other parts of the organization, someone would have cut me off, so I just go ahead, do my own thing, without asking them.

These quotes indicated that the organization did not encourage working across units. In fact, it had created barriers that prevented people from working across departments. Rarely did any efforts to collaborate survive in this kind of environment.

Recognition of Problems and Strengths

The last observation was encouraging. It was how the staff reacted to the current situation. Again, we use quotes from middle managers to illustrate.

> We have to start addressing these tough problems. We have to quit pretending we can operate the way we did in the past, keeping the middle of the organization in a hole. We've got to make some changes, let's get on with it.

> We are good. We are very good. I don't care what measure you use. But we are just not performing up to par. There are organizational and cultural barriers that interfere. We need to be able to work together across units. Let's do this. If we can accomplish better teamwork, our company can do better than any other company on the face of this earth.

> We hire very good people, who want to do a good job. What we do is we bury them within the functional organization and don't let them do it. Our middle managers are suffocated.

> We've got the horsepower to solve the problems. Let the people who need to work together do that.

> We've got a million ideas in this company. Turn us loose. Right now we're being cut off, walled off, and prevented from working together to get those ideas into practice.

It is very clear that the people saw there was a lot of work to be done. At the same time, there was tremendous pride in the company and a recognition that there was a lot of strength to build on. The people were willing to work hard and become involved in order to solve the problems, and so that's what we were going to give them the opportunity to do.

We presented our findings, data, and quotes to David Frank and his staff of vice presidents, all of whom shook their heads in disbelief. At the same time, they acknowledged that the findings were on target. While it was hard for them to accept that they had allowed the organization to become this way, it was possible for them to see that there were major problems. They knew something needed to be done to unblock their middle managers. At the end of the presentation of the results, the atmosphere in the room was one of resignation. Top management was resigned to dealing with the problems that they knew must be dealt with if the company was to survive. They also recognized that the problems would be very difficult, for they would require changes in well-established habits and practices.

To the reader: We return to EMI in Chap. 7 to describe the changes they undertook in order to tackle these challenges, and we revisit EMI in the Epilogue to describe the results two years later. We have introduced EMI to the reader now in order to give an example of the situation we discuss in the next several chapters.

PART 1
The Gap in the Middle

1
Why Middle Managers Matter

Many people call [middle managers] the concrete layer and tell endless stories of how they get in the way of progress.
—LEONARD SCHLESINGER AND JAMES HESKETT
Harvard Business Review[1]

After all, who wants middle managers if what they do is block information from those closest to the action who need it most to run the business fast.
—TOM PETERS

Middle managers are the key for GE's growth over the years ahead.
JACK WELCH
CEO, General Electric

Amid all the dramatic and unforeseen changes in the world order that have occurred in the last few years, perhaps the one with most lasting impact is the changing face of international economic competition. As a result of what we call the New Competitive Reality, firms everywhere around the world are struggling to survive in a game where the rules seem to be in a state of continuous flux.

Fortress America firms, like General Motors and IBM, that long dominated their markets have had to take drastic measures to ensure their own survival. As they and other U.S. firms try to come to grips with today's New Competitive Reality, their focus is on cutting costs by closing plants and laying off employees. In company after company, we have found that these moves to become "lean and mean" are having the biggest impact on middle managers. In many firms, middle managers are the scapegoats for their company's loss of competitive position.

As the comments at the beginning of this chapter suggest, *there is no clear-cut consensus about the future place of middle managers in American organizations*. Indeed, some have raised the question whether middle managers are needed at all. They are seen as "concrete layers" getting in the way of progress.

This debate reflects the pressures of the New Competitive Reality faced by American organizations today. The impact of the new competitive environment is not limited to giant American corporations like Caterpillar, IBM, General Electric, and General Motors. Around the world, managers of virtually every firm—regardless of its size—are well aware that they are now in a new ball game and that the names and numbers of the players have changed.

The New Competitive Reality

To begin, we discuss how the New Competitive Reality developed during the 1980s—and how the pressures it caused have changed the jobs of middle managers. Over the past decade, the rules have been rewritten because of three fundamental changes in the competitive environment: deregulation, global competition, and further intensification of the pressure for short-term results.

1. *Deregulation* has blurred the market boundaries that traditionally separated one industry from another. For instance, in the financial arena over the past decade old lines of demarcation have become blurred almost beyond recognition. Fidelity Financial Services, a tour de force in mutual funds, has entered the securities brokerage business; brokerage firms like A. G. Edwards are selling insurance; and insurance firms like The New England and Metropolitan are major factors in portfolio management. American Express is in all these segments competing with everyone, and the commercial banks are hot on their heels.

It has also been a decade full of realignments and broad change for other industries, such as health care, airlines, railroads, and trucking. And more basic changes are on the horizon for people in these and other fields.

2. *Global Competition* has blurred the significance of international boundaries as well. Foreign companies have invaded virtually every corner of American markets, just as U.S. firms moved into Europe after World War II. For instance, while American investment firms like Salomon Brothers and Morgan Stanley were establishing significant positions in London and Tokyo, Credit Suisse was increasing its investment in its American affiliate (First Boston). Moving beyond its home base in Tokyo, Nomura Securities has established a fully staffed, state-of-the-art investment capability in New York.

In many instances, overseas competitors produce more technologically advanced and higher-quality products than do their American counterparts. Although U.S. firms have made improvements, many have not yet caught up. For example, despite a major effort to improve quality, American carmakers still lag behind. In each of the past five years foreign makes have occupied most of the top 10 places in the J. D. Power Customer Satisfaction ratings. Moreover, several of these top-quality models— from Japanese firms like Honda—are actually manufactured in plants located in the United States.

Globalization goes beyond just having more competitors. It means that a firm needs to be a global company, to be a world-class competitor wherever markets exist. It requires understanding differences among markets, as well as being at the forefront of new product technology and manufacturing efficiencies.

3. *Pressure for short-term results* hangs over the heads of senior managers and diverts their attention away from long-term performance. They are under the gun to report favorable earnings every three months. This pressure has increased with the changing ownership of a firm's shares. In the 1980s, the top management of several companies whose stock was lagging in the market found themselves the targets of raids by Boone Pickens, Asher Edelman, Carl Icahn, or Harold Simmons.

While the names of these raiders have largely faded from the headlines, far more important and sustainable pressure on corporate managements is being exerted by pension funds and other major institutional investors, who—collectively—often own over one-half of a firm's shares. Long passive investors, this group has begun to flex its muscles. They, too, are under pressure to produce superior short-term results in the portfolios under their supervision.

Fifteen years ago when General Motors was dominating the American auto market, the company's shareholders were a content group, enjoying high dividends and happy with the company's performance. By the mid-1980s, this shareholder complacency had changed. Large pension funds—led by the State of California and New York City—became increasingly vocal as the company's results lagged. In the press and at meetings with Wall Street analysts, they pilloried Roger Smith about GM's shortcomings. In 1992, they successfully pressured the "outside" members of the Board to intervene directly in GM's top management structure.

In many corporations, pension funds have become a cost center. If investment returns exceed certain assumptions, a firm can elect to cut its costs by reducing the size of its pension contribution. In turn, this cost reduction flows through to improved earnings. It is not surprising, then, that pension-fund investment managers discovered that the way to keep their pension-fund clients happy was to produce favorable short-term results.

If a company's quarterly earnings fall short of the expectations of Wall Street security analysts, its shares may drop sharply in a few minutes as this information is instantly transmitted to investors across the country. Adding to this pressure, in most American companies the bonuses and stock options of senior managers are based upon the firm's profits for the latest year. Top managers in America are paid much larger salaries than is the case in Asia and Europe, and the desire to keep compensation high further adds to the pressure to report favorable quarterly earnings.

Our global competitors do not have their attention focused so intently on short-term profits and the accompanying fluctuations in their company's stock price. In Europe and Asia, investors do not pay such single-minded attention to interim earnings reports. As a result, managements abroad are able to plan and manage for the long term. We need more of this kind of thinking rather than what we describe next.

Merge, Purge, and Leverage: Not the Long-Term Answer

These three factors—deregulation, globalization, and short-term financial pressure—have permanently changed the size of the playing field and altered the rules of the ball game for American corporations. The pressures of the New Competitive Reality have forced many companies to make changes in what they had previously considered sound operating practices.

The first response of American corporations was focused on taking steps to cut operating costs. Phrases such as "restructuring" and "downsizing" were used to describe this process. So far, the most common remedies have entailed doing more with less, such as:

- Rationalizing capacity by closing surplus and inefficient plants,
- Reducing headcounts,
- Adopting just-in-time systems to cut the costs of carrying inventory,
- Selling or dropping unprofitable lines of business, and
- Trying to create a sense of urgency in the organization toward the challenge presented by the tougher competitive struggle.

For many companies, the principal actions of the recovery strategy were initiated under the looming threat of an unfriendly takeover. In reality, top management's recovery strategy was actually a survival strategy. If they lost control of the company in a merger, their jobs would be in jeopardy . In response, they scrambled to boost their profits as quickly as possible. This desire to achieve quick results is understandable, but it falls short of what a firm needs to do to keep ahead of its competitors in the long run.

Downsizing, another common form of cost cutting, is a prescription for short-term remedies that does not address the causes of the long-term illness. Leveraged buyouts (LBOs) are not a strategy for restoring competitiveness. Instead, LBOs are just the sort of short-term financial opportunism that contributes to a decline in competitiveness.

Actions to merge, purge, and leverage result in less growth, not more. They miss the point. When they finish downsizing and restructuring, American managers will not have addressed the long-term problems they face in today's New Competitive Reality. Instead, the key to sustainable progress in the long run is for American firms to become world-class competitors.

Strategies of World-Class Competitors

World-class competitors base their strategies on more than a narrow, short-term approach. Their focus is not on downsizing to meet the next payment on junk bonds. Instead, they concentrate on taking steps to create new products and on increasing their market share. They strive to establish and preserve a competitive advantage by developing the capabilities to:

- Invest in new technology;
- Anticipate changes in individual, indigenous market segments;
- Introduce innovative new products that keep a firm *ahead* of international competitors;
- Manage the growing complexities of being truly global, such as geographically dispersed manufacturing facilities and joint ventures with international partners; and
- Produce products and provide services that meet world-class quality standards.

These are the proven capabilities of organizations that are meeting the demands of the New Competitive Reality. These capabilities will be only a pipe dream for companies that do not understand the importance of their middle managers in their efforts to be world-class competitors. Some firms clearly recognize their essential role. For instance, Procter & Gamble has restructured its approach to marketing its individual brands, giving middle managers control and responsibility for a group of products. Other illustrations of firms that have responded to these new requirements of competitiveness are GE, Merck, Corning, and H. J. Heinz. The senior managers of these companies understand the necessity for delegating important decision-making authority to cross-functional teams of middle managers.

In a nutshell, *we believe senior managers must think of middle managers not as obstacles but, instead, as the source of the capabilities their company needs to be a full-fledged international competitor.* In our view, the long-term approach to true global competitiveness lies in taking middle managers out of their traditional roles and giving them new responsibilities. *Functioning in new roles, middle managers hold the key to global competitiveness.* Middle managers represent a resource that is underutilized, a resource that can be redirected to help American firms gain the capabilities of world-class competitors.

Many firms are not capitalizing on the potential of their middle management. A deep-seated reason U.S. corporations have become less competitive is that American middle managers are not functioning effectively. In the early 1980s we first became aware of the extent of discontent among middle managers. Through our continuing research in organization after organization we have found that:

- Middle managers have lost the willingness to take risks.

- They are hesitant to innovate.

- They are reluctant to seize the opportunity when senior management tries to delegate decisions to them.

- They focus on defending their turf, so information sharing and communication among departments are ineffective. *Within* the firm, competition often supersedes teamwork.

In the chapters that follow, we show how middle managers are falling short of their potential to make a major difference in their company's competitiveness.

Frustration in the Middle and at the Top

In our experience with firms ranging from Aerodyne with annual sales of $5 million to General Motors with revenues of $120 billion, it is clear that many of the efforts to increase the commitment and effectiveness of middle managers have fallen short.

In many firms, senior managers decided to shift the power to decide about everyday operations to middle managers, who are closer to the operations and to the customer. This common move to decentralize, which was popularized by Tom Peters and Bob Waterman,[2] is based on the principle that involvement, participation, empowerment, and ownership motivate people. As a result, senior managers expected that middle managers would rise to the challenge and enthusiastically accept their new responsibilities.

As we evaluate these efforts today, however, we see many attempts to delegate operational responsibilities that are not working. Vertical channels are still clogged, decisions are not being made any faster, and foreign competitors can still introduce products faster than American firms can.

Frustration is mounting—in the middle and at the top. A senior manager made these observations to us about his three-year effort to delegate decisions to his middle managers:

> The people just don't want it. They say they don't know what to do. In fact, I think they are actually afraid of the risk; it's safer for them not to have to make decisions and be held accountable.

At the same time, discontent is clear among middle managers as well. The following comment made by an individual in another firm reflects this view:

> Management tells us they want to move decisions down to our level. It's just lip service. The first time we determined which outside supplier to use, our bosses reversed our decision, saying that we were unaware of a critical factor—there were provisions in the labor agreement with the unions that restricted our ability to outsource those parts. Why didn't they give us the full picture in the first place?

So far much of this discussion has been about how the broad trends in the *external* environment are affecting American firms and the middle managers in them. Now, we want to shift our attention to the internal environment in organizations where changes are causing discontent and frustration for middle managers.

The Days of the Warlords Are Over

In the 1960s and early 1970s, the number of middle managers in most organizations grew at a rapid rate.[3] One estimate suggests that their ranks grew fivefold between 1950 and 1975. By 1980, it is estimated that middle managers made up 10 percent of the U.S. work force, over twice the comparable rate in Japan. The number of organizational layers multiplied like wildfire, reaching more than 100 at some large U.S. firms.

To deal with the growing complexities of operations, senior management added middle managers to their staffs. As these fiefdoms expanded, so did the volume of analyses and reports they produced. Middle managers functioned in vertical roles. They were message carriers. Senior managers expected them to pass the word to those in the lower ranks who, in turn, had messages they wanted senior managers to hear.

Their roles and responsibilities were supervisory, controlling the vertical flow of directions and information within departmental channels. They compiled data and prepared reports for those at the top.

Now, however, their numbers are shrinking. In the 1980s when the competitive heat intensified and cost cutting became essential to survival, it is not surprising that senior managers started to question why they needed so many reports and whether such large staffs were necessary. Fiefdoms and warlords were out. Lean and mean was in.

Middle managers have been major targets of the resulting purge and merge and restructure and leverage process. They have been the principal scapegoats of downsizing—restructuring, delayering, rationalizing—whatever people chose to call the effort to become lean and mean. Regardless of the semantics, the most severe impact has been on middle managers. In many firms, their ranks are decimated.

According to one study, one-third of all middle-management jobs were lost in the purge.[4] Another analysis showed that from 1979 to 1987 more than 1,000,000 middle managers and staff professionals lost their jobs. The pace has not let up since. Between 1987 and 1991, more than three-quarters of the Fortune 1000 firms reduced the number of middle managers.

Catch-22 in the Middle

Downsizing is the most visible, but it is not the only aspect of the New Competitive Reality that is affecting middle management. Indeed, we were not surprised to find frustrated middle managers at firms that were downsizing. *However, we were surprised that this same discontent was also clear at firms that were expanding rapidly.* At these organizations, the ranks of middle managers were still growing, not contracting. As their firms continued to expand, these middle managers looked forward to the prospect of additional promotions. Clearly, there were other factors besides downsizing and layoffs contributing to the frustration in the middle.

Looking further, some aspects of today's competitive environment are making the work of middle managers more difficult and are restricting their ability to function effectively. Among these factors are the growing complexity of cross-functional coordination, shorter time frames, increased reliance on data-based information systems, and organizational downsizing.

The Growing Complexity of Cross-Functional Coordination

As business becomes more global, international firms are scrambling to enter new markets in many different countries. It is not just large, highly visible firms such as Coca-Cola, Colgate, IBM, and McDonalds that are global. In addition, as Peter Drucker has observed, even middle-sized U.S. firms have found that they must compete around the world in order to survive.

Joint arrangements have mushroomed in popularity as a means of entering a new market overseas. On any given day, the financial section of the newspaper normally has an announcement of a new alliance between international partners. These allegiances encompass a wide spectrum of variations, including equity participation, investments, licensing agreements, research and marketing combinations, joint ventures, and mergers.

International combinations are on the rise in industry after industry. In the pharmaceutical field, for instance, these arrangements have taken a variety of forms. One recent megacombination involved a merger between Beacham in England and SmithKline in America. In addition, Roche, the Swiss firm, has acquired a 60 percent interest in Genentech, with an option to acquire the remaining 40 percent. Eastman Kodak's Sterling Drug unit is exploring a joint venture with Sanofi, a leading French pharmaceutical firm. In another increasingly common arrangement, Merck and Du Pont have set up a joint venture for sharing the results of their medical research.

Elsewhere, in 1989 Waste Management purchased Sellbergs, a leading solid and hazardous waste disposal firm in Sweden and Spain, in order to capitalize on the opportunities it expects to develop in Europe after 1992. Also, at GMFanuc Robotics, which began as a joint venture of General Motors and Fanuc and is now wholly owned by Fanuc (a Japanese manufacturer), the task of international coordination is complex indeed. For example:

- Research and development are conducted in Japan and in the United States.

- Marketing is located in the United States and Europe.

- Components are manufactured both in Japan and in the United States. Final assembly is done in the United States.

- Customer support services are based in the United States and Europe.

At GMFanuc, the principal coordinators of this complex enterprise are middle managers scattered around the world who must understand different cultures and be able to communicate clearly despite wide language and cultural differences. The key to success in this field—as in many others—is the ability to move new technologies through the development process and on to the market more rapidly than competitors. At the same time, managers must strive to meet world-class quality standards.

There are also other changes that have added to the complexities of the operating responsibilities of middle managers. Many firms have undertaken new relationships with customers and suppliers who are often considered to be outside traditional organizational boundaries. Following the long-standing practice in Japan, suppliers in the United States are becoming more involved in the core activities of their customers. The reverse pattern is true as well, i.e., customers are getting more involved in the operations of their suppliers.

To improve coordination and speed up the process of developing new models, American auto firms have introduced a procedure called "simultaneous engineering." At the heart of this process is a series of cross-functional teams—called Product Development Teams—which commonly include an outside supplier who will produce a specific part for a new model.

Further, to alter what had long been an arm's-length, frequently dictatorial approach to suppliers, some companies have developed partnership arrangements with their suppliers. One example is Ray Campbell at General Motors, who in 1985 provided the impetus for the creation of a joint Suppliers Council with representatives of outside suppliers who can speak their minds freely. The purpose of the Council is to initiate new approaches for working more effectively together.

Frequently, this approach requires that middle managers function in an entirely different way. For example, a buyer may have to stop dictating terms and prices and learn to treat a supplier as a partner. This collaborative process requires a higher level of interaction and cooperation with individuals outside their own corporate organization.

These new outside arrangements are not limited to suppliers. Traditional relationships with customers are changing as well. For example, many customers now have direct access to the production floor. People with production assignments at Armco Steel now make regular visits to their customers' facilities to discuss current problems and assess future needs.

As a result, the middle managers responsible for coordinating the functional complexities of these interactions are working with, and dependent upon, a significantly greater number of people, both inside and outside their organizations. These individuals are often great distances away, and they may even speak a different language and belong to a different culture.

Shorter Time Frames

Accelerating technological change has made it difficult for everyone, especially middle managers, to keep up. The education and training needed to retain technical competence require a lot of time and effort.

Further, as a result of added international competition, the new product cycle is getting shorter and shorter. In many areas, U.S. firms still lag behind their Japanese competitors. For instance, while it took General Motors five years from conception to introduction of the Pontiac Fiero that hit the market in 1983, the world-class standard is much shorter. It took Toyota only 2½ years to respond to the Fiero with the MR-2 model.

On the other hand, Digital Equipment is an example of a U.S. company that has successfully reduced the new product cycle. In 1980 it took Digital about three years on average to introduce a computer. By 1985, the firm cut the required time in half. Another illustration of a global firm that has cut the time for introducing a product is Land Rover in England. In 1989 Land Rover introduced a new model, the Discovery, that took less than three years to develop.

In most instances, middle managers have the responsibility for shepherding new products onto the market. Perhaps the plural—markets—is more appropriate in today's global environment. In 1989 Gillette successfully launched its new Sensor razor simultaneously in 18 major markets throughout the world. To keep ahead of overseas competitors, middle managers at firms like Gillette are today under pressure to speed up the new product cycle.

In facing this New Competitive Reality, the ability to market new products more rapidly than the competition has become the lifeline of survival. To further complicate the matter, middle managers must now meet stricter quality standards and produce items of world-class quality— beginning at the time of product launch. Today's world-class standards mean doing it right the first time.

Increased Reliance on Data-Based Information Systems

As companies have replaced people networks with data networks as the means for gathering and disseminating information, middle managers often do not get the vital qualitative information they need. Although they get the figures on the performance of their unit versus budget, they commonly lack good measures of people's job satisfaction and attitudes. Often we found that issues involving people—such as a lack of understanding of the firm's goals or a failure to appreciate the urgency of responding quickly to competitive pressures—are responsible for the problems blocking what many middle managers are trying to accomplish.

The idea that "everything comes out in the numbers" reflects the short-term thinking that now dominates American management. In many firms, the predominant view is that quantitative data is "hard" and therefore important. But communication and information sharing among people are not quantifiable, so they are "soft" and hence not important.

Pressed for time, many middle and senior managers have become overreliant on computer output as their primary source of information. We have talked with many middle managers who rely heavily on their printouts to give them a picture of what is happening. We have seen them become increasingly isolated—from people in other parts of their firms, from the factory floor, and from their customers in supermarkets and showrooms.

Organizational Downsizing

As we have already indicated, pressure from competitors and financial raiders has forced many managements to restructure and reduce the size of their staffs. The extensive reduction in the ranks of middle managers has resulted in a greater burden on those remaining. In many instances, their responsibilities have increased. *They are being asked to do more, to do it better, faster, and with less. As we have pointed out, although downsizing has received most of the attention, it is just one of several factors that have resulted in a major increase in the demands placed on middle managers.*

A Changed World

We have described the changes that have altered the world of middle managers. The changes are both external and internal, and we can diagram their impact on middle managers as shown in Fig. 1.1.

To change this picture, companies need to move ahead in a new direction to capture the commitment of the smaller core of middle managers who remain. After all, as one senior manager told us, "they are the people who really do the work around here."

External Changes	Impact on Middle Managers
Deregulation	Unwilling to take risks
Global competition	Reluctant to innovate
Pressure for short-term results	Wary of accepting new responsibilities
Internal Changes	Confused about goals
Growing functional complexity	Must do more, better, faster, with less
Shorter time frames	
Reliance on data networks	Feeling stress
Downsizing	Discontented
	Frustrated

Figure 1.1. A changed world for middle managers.

The Key to Growth

The recovery in American competitiveness won't last without middle management on board. They hold the keys to the effort to manage the functional complexities of global operations, to maintain a line of state-of-the-art products, to shorten the time required in the new product cycle, and to offer products that meet world-class quality standards.

Sustaining competitiveness today involves much more than cutting costs and downsizing. Beyond these elements, global leadership requires world-class quality, pioneering technology, and an accelerated new-product cycle. These elements of competitive advantage go far beyond reducing costs. Rather, they focus attention on growth and market leadership. It's a harder task to put a firm back on an upward growth curve than it was to downsize. However, as we have indicated, the ability to grow profitably and increase market share are the real measures of a firm's capacity to meet the test of the New Competitive Reality.

In the early 1980s, Xerox faced a daunting challenge when Canon introduced a small copier at a price of $1000—a fraction of the $10,000 price of Xerox's bottom-of-the-line machine. Rather than attempt to cut the cost by substituting cheaper materials and reducing the quality of the $10,000 machine, engineers at Xerox went back to the drawing board and started from scratch. Using a new approach, they were able to produce a small-end machine that was fully competitive with Canon's. Xerox not only countered the competitive threat, but was also able to increase its share of this rapidly growing segment of the market.

General Electric is an example of a firm that has been through both the cost-cutting and the growth phases of this process as it has struggled to sustain its competitive position. In 1984, after Jack Welch took over at GE from Reg Jones, his first actions were to reduce the company's size. He sold several divisions, including Utah International, which had been one of Jones's prize acquisitions. Welch's message was direct and unmistakable: General Electric would be either #1 or #2 in a business, or they would get out.

Welch slashed costs through layoffs, restructuring, asset sales, and plant closings. He attacked what he considered a bloated bureaucracy. In the process, he laid off thousands of middle managers. Soon he was known around GE as "Neutron Jack."

Yet, it is now clear that Welch's efforts to transform GE have entered a second, very different phase. He has shifted his emphasis to the development of the capabilities of his middle managers. He has strengthened the company's management training center at Crotonville, New York. He is personally involved with every class of managers that goes through Crotonville.

In Welch's view, the key to the future growth in GE's productivity is to "liberate" and "empower" the company's middle managers. Even after Welch's staff reductions, there are still 100,000 middle managers and staff professionals at GE, representing one-third of total employment.[5] Many of these managers began their careers at GE during the "age of the warlords" in the 1960s and 1970s. On average, they joined the firm five years before Welch became CEO, during a less competitive time for American industry. In the face of all the staff cuts, it won't be easy for those middle managers who remain to become believers in the new GE Welch is constructing. This challenge for Welch is greater than downsizing, but he recognizes that these middle managers are the key to GE's future competitiveness and vitality.

For years, Lee Iacocca's style at Chrysler was top-down, with little decision making taking place down in the ranks of the organization. Costs rose, and the company hadn't had a high-volume new-product success since the Voyager minivan, introduced in 1984. Today, once again fighting for its survival, Chrysler has taken action to improve its product-development process. The new Viper, a limited-production sports car, took only 2½ years to develop. Also, in the creation of the new LH series—the replacement for the decade-old K-cars—Iacocca broke precedent and delegated complete authority to the project leader, Glenn Gardner. Gardner set out to cut red tape and completely overhaul the way Chrysler develops new models. In the process, he has used fewer people and sharply reduced the product-development cycle for this new line that is so vital to Chrysler's survival.[6]

In the next chapter, we discuss the background of our interest in middle managers and what we found in our review of past studies about them. We found that the results in these studies were not consistent with what we discovered was actually happening in the companies where we were working. As a result, we decided to conduct our own assessment. In the end, this study (described in Chap. 3) helped us understand a great deal more about middle managers and the causes of their discontent and ineffectiveness.

Endnotes

1. Leonard A. Schlesinger and James L. Heskett, "The Service-Driven Service Company," *Harvard Business Review*, September-October 1991, Vol. 69, No. 5, p. 81.

   The quote by Tom Peters is from an excellent Public Broadcasting System/Excel series called "Thriving on Chaos," which aired during December 1989.

   The comment about middle managers by Jack Welch is from an article by Thomas A. Stewart entitled "GE Keeps Those Ideas Coming" that appeared in *Fortune*, August 12, 1991.

2. Thomas J. Peters and Robert H. Waterman, Jr., *In Search of Excellence*, New York: Harper and Row, 1982. Although criticized in some quarters for lack of rigor, we believe that this book has had a major impact in helping many American managers develop a blueprint for improved competitiveness.

3. For a discussion of these trends, see Judith M. Bardwick, *The Plateauing Trap*, New York: AMACOM, 1986, and Kim S. Cameron, Sarah J. Freeman, and Aneil K. Mishara, "Best Practices in White-Collar Downsizing: Managing Contradictions," *Academy of Management Executive*, 1991, Vol. 5. No. 3.

4. See Charles Handy, *The Age of Unreason*, Cambridge, MA: Harvard Business School Press, 1989, p. 91. Handy, a British professor, consultant and writer is one of the best forward-looking thinkers. This book is up to his usual high standard.

5. Thomas A. Stewart, "GE Keeps Those Ideas Coming," *Fortune*, August 12, 1991.

6. Joseph B. White, Gregory A. Patterson, and Paul Ingrassia, "Long Road Ahead: American Auto Makers Need Major Overhaul to Match the Japanese," *The Wall Street Journal*, January 10, 1992.

   Because of our consulting activities and general enthusiasm for cars, we read several auto industry magazines to keep up on what's new in the field. We are particularly partial to *Automobile*—it's snappily written and very opinionated. For a description of the development of the Viper, see Jean Lindamood's article in the November 1991 *Automobile*, entitled "The Very First Viper RT/10 Drive."

2

The Conventional Wisdom: Hear No Gap, See No Gap

By the mid-1980s, our consulting work led us to believe there was a gap in the middle of many organizations. We began using the term *gap in the middle* as shorthand for the greater amount of frustration and discontent we were finding among middle managers than among people at levels just above *and* below them.

What we wanted to find out was straightforward:

1. Is there a gap today at the middle-manager level in different types of organizations?
2. If a gap does exist, what are its principal causes?

Researching Current Literature

To begin our exploration, we turned to the management literature to see if a gap in the middle was evident from past research in areas such as job satisfaction and organizational commitment. We wanted to see if past studies had identified any evidence of a significant amount of job dissatisfaction or a lack of organizational commitment at the middle-manager level.

What we found surprised us. To begin with, we discovered that most researchers had not attempted to find out whether people at different levels in an organization felt differently about job satisfaction, for example. In fact, most of the research was based upon attitudes of people at only one level.

Moreover, in the limited number of studies that did include organizational level, we did not find evidence of unusual discontent and frustration among middle managers.

For instance, in a classic study, *Personality and Organization,* Chris Argyris suggested that there is a direct relationship between the satisfaction of a person's needs and his or her level in the firm.[1] In other words, Argyris found that the higher a person was in the organization, the better he or she could satisfy personal higher-order needs, such as self-esteem and self-actualization.

Although the focus of most research studies was on other variables such as age, length of service, and family size, Argyris's findings were also supported in the few quantitative studies that included organizational level.

Two studies using survey, or quantitative data, are noteworthy because the participants included people from all levels of an organization, from unskilled workers at the bottom to senior managers at the top. Hulin and Smith's study in 1965 included 185 men and 85 women from two manufacturing plants in New England. A later survey in the mid-1970s by Adams, Laker, and Hulin involved people classified into 20 organizational levels in a packing plant in the Midwest.[2]

These studies demonstrated, for example, that job satisfaction was higher for people at each successive step in the organizational ladder. The typical pattern suggested by this research could be illustrated as shown in Fig. 2.1.

The conclusion of these studies was clear. The higher you were in a company, the more satisfied you were with your job.

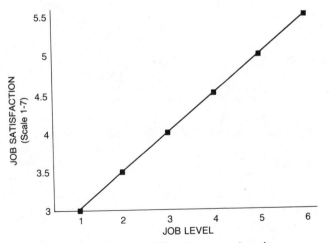

Figure 2.1. Typical pattern of data from research studies.

Moving beyond job satisfaction, we also found that these studies showed a similar pattern existing in the relationship between organizational commitment and organizational level. Again, the higher a person's rank in a firm, the more committed he or she is to the organization itself. In other words, commitment is greater at each successively higher level.

There were a few exceptions to this pattern of results, such as those from a study in the late 1960s of the U.S. Forest Service. Hall, Schneider, and Nygren found that the relationship between commitment and level was not as consistent as other studies had suggested.[3] In this study, there is a suggestion of a gap in the middle ranks. However, because of the limited number of participants, the relatively small differences in the results among different levels were not conclusive.

In summary, most of the people conducting these studies hadn't looked for differences in attitudes at different levels in an organization. Those who did failed to find much evidence of an unusual amount of discontent among middle managers. As a result, based on the conventional wisdom, the answer to our first question seemed clear: There was little evidence of a gap in the middle.

Is the Conventional Wisdom Out-of-Date?

As we have indicated, we found a number of limitations in this research. Most of the studies were of just one organization, or they didn't include a full range of levels from the bottom to the top. In addition, the number of people involved in a study was often not large enough for the results to be conclusive.

Our most significant reservation, however, was that the studies in the literature might be out of date. They were conducted between 1945 and 1970. As we indicated in the previous chapter, this period represented a time when middle managers were riding high. Their numbers were increasing, and the competitive environment for American companies was far more benign than is the case today.

Jeffrey Pfeffer, a widely respected organizational researcher from Stanford, has suggested that people engaged in research must understand that changes in demographics, economics, and social factors may lead to different results from one period to another.[4] In this case, we wondered if the findings from these past studies would hold up in today's more competitive environment where middle managers face pressures and challenges unknown to their cohorts just a few years ago.

Although there were no recent quantitative studies that might have identified problems among middle managers, a few students of organizations were noticing the same type of discontent among middle managers that we had observed.

From the perspective of those at the top of the pyramid, Paul Lawrence at Harvard has pointed to a "blockage" in the middle of organizations that was frustrating senior managers' efforts to implement strategy.[5]

In addition, the individual who has most consistently addressed himself to "middles" is Barry Oshry, a Boston-based former professor at Boston University.[6] Oshry has focused his attention on the problems that "middles" have served as the messengers between the "tops" and the "workers."

In our explorations it soon became apparent that the lack of current studies with comprehensive, quantitative information was holding us back from identifying and understanding the nature of this problem. Further, if the gap did exist, we needed to explore its causes in order to understand its full impact.

What we needed was "fresh" survey data from people in several different types of companies. Since the environment in the organizations studied during the 1945–1970 period didn't fit our impressions of the reality facing middle managers today, we decided that we needed our own hard data to find out whether a gap was present in organizations.

In preparing to do our study, we needed to develop a conceptual framework of the potential causes of the gap—if, in fact, it did exist. We knew that we would need to identify the causes in order to decide the steps both senior and middle managers could take to enable middle managers to function more effectively.

Consequently, we next turn to our second question: What are the possible causes of a gap among middle managers?

Possible Causes for the Gap, Round 1

In formulating a framework for addressing this question, we decided to explore two approaches for identifying factors that might be related to the gap:

1. Individual factors such as career plateauing at midlife; and

2. Organizational factors such as deficiencies in structure and procedures.

To begin with, we thought one potential cause was career plateauing, faced by middle managers who are at the midpoint in their lives and careers.

Before considering the notion of "the midlife crisis" that was popularized by Gail Sheehy in *Passages* in the late seventies, we first briefly review what past studies have noted as the relationship between age and such issues as job satisfaction.[7]

In the studies examining these relationships, no clear-cut pattern is evident. Most of the studies found that, as an individual gets older, his or her job satisfaction increases. However, in the most extensive study of more than 10,000 managers in a merchandising firm conducted in the early 1970s, researchers did not find a consistent pattern.[8] The most satisfied were those managers who had been with the firm for the shortest and longest periods, while those who had an average length of service were noticeably less satisfied.

Similarly, in a smaller study at this same time, Mary Sheldon was surprised to find a lower level of commitment among people in the middle ranks with an average length of service.[9] Later, in attempting to explain Sheldon's unexpected findings, Gerry Salancik speculated that the most committed among Sheldon's middle group were those individuals with a short time in the company who have a clear sense of where they are going *and* those with a long time of service who are still middle managers.[10]

Salancik suggests that middle managers who have been in a company long time are reconciled to the fact that they are not going to be promoted any further. For those people in the middle ranks with an average length of service, however, the level of commitment is low because they are uncertain of their future and whether they will be promoted. Salancik's explanation as well as the discussion related to adult and career development that follows suggests that the discontent and frustration of middle managers could result from reaching a career plateau in middle age.

Our aim is not to provide an extensive review of everything academics have written about career plateauing. Rather, our purpose is to explain why we wanted to find out in our study if there is a clear connection between career plateauing and the discontent on the part of middle managers.

Passages Revisited

One approach to understanding adult and career development that we felt might explain the gap involved career-stage models that became popular in the 1960s and 1970s. This approach suggested that people proceed through a series of clearly separate stages in their careers, marked by shifts in their needs.

Once the idea of career stages was introduced, researchers soon began to focus on the midlife stage that men experienced in midcareer. (All the initial studies involved only men!) One of the first to focus on managers in midcareer was Harry Levinson.[11] In a 1969 article, Levinson suggested that as managers reach middle age they face a developmental crisis that may result in changes, not only in their health, lifestyle, and family relationships, but also in their career aspirations.

Levinson said that the middle years were a time of career crisis as managers tried to come to terms with the realization that, in all likelihood, they have already received their final promotion.

The most detailed and most controversial study of adult developmental stages was conducted in the 1970s by Daniel Levinson (no relation to Harry) and his colleagues at Yale.[12] Daniel Levinson's study was of the lives of 40 men—only men, which is the source of some of the controversy. Gail Sheehy based her best-seller, *Passages*, on the data from this study.

Levinson concluded that a man's life evolves through a set sequence of stages in his adult years. The sequence consists of a series of 15-year stable periods, with 5-year transition periods interspersed in between. The 5-year transitions are a time of intense reflection and, frequently, tumultuous struggles within the individual and with those in the "outside" world.

Career Plateauing at Midlife

The one of Levinson's stages that is of particular interest to our study is the midlife transition. Levinson says that this transition begins at age 40 or 41 and lasts for five years. These career-stage theories suggest that the gap might be especially clear for middle managers at midlife who are experiencing personal struggles and self-doubt. Levinson's work suggests that this is common behavior at this life stage.

Taking a somewhat different slant, in the mid-1970s Tim Hall, who is now at Boston University, and Edgar Schein, from the Sloan School at MIT, broadened the view beyond the *individual* factors to focus on the *organizational* aspects of career plateauing.[13] They said that middle managers might be "organizationally or structurally plateaued" as opposed to being "personally plateaued."

This approach suggests that career plateauing results from a lack of opportunities for further promotion as a manager moves up in the narrowing pyramid. Schein noted that the likelihood that each promotion will be the last increases with each step upward. The problem was not with the individual, but with the diminishing geometry of promotions. There are simply fewer positions at the top of the pyramid than there are in the middle.

While career plateauing might explain why there would be discontent and frustration at the middle-manager level, one question was unanswered: If midlife transitions did in fact exist, why wasn't the gap at the middle-manager level clear in the studies that we mentioned earlier in this chapter?

The explanation that made sense to us was one that we have alluded to already: The gap was not apparent from the studies we found in our search of the literature because they were out of date. They were measuring people's views and attitudes during a time when the competitive world was less demanding.

Judith Bardwick, who has focused much of her academic and clinical work as a psychologist on career development, agrees with this view.[14] She suggests that people in organizations, especially at the middle-manager level, face a different environment today than in the period from 1950 to 1980. Her work raises the possibility that the gap among middle managers is a new, contemporary phenomenon.

The research on job satisfaction and organizational commitment mentioned earlier took place during a period of strong economic growth in the United States and a less competitive environment. During this time, the ranks of middle managers were growing, and promotions were coming frequently. The warlords we mentioned in Chap. 1 could increase the size of their fiefdoms because their organizations were expanding.

However, as we described in Chap. 1, the less demanding competitive environment of their earlier period has been replaced by a New Competitive Reality. The resulting restructuring and downsizing have resulted in disproportionately large reductions in the ranks of middle managers.

Next, we shift our attention from individual to organizational factors that may account for the gap. A second possible cause concerns shortcomings in the structure and practices in organizations.

Possible Causes for the Gap, Round 2

An additional, or alternative, explanation is that the gap is a result of poor lateral integration across departments. In this view, the gap is caused by a lack of effective cross-functional communication, cooperation, and teamwork at the middle-manager level.

Earlier we mentioned Barry Oshry, who has called attention to the difficulties faced by people in the middle ranks.[15] Oshry thinks that middle managers incorrectly hold themselves to blame for the frustration and discontent they experience. Instead, he believes that shortcomings of the organization itself are at fault.

What are these organizational deficiencies? Oshry points to the inability of middle managers to perform laterally, that is, in integrative roles linking and communicating across departmental lines with their peers in other functional areas.

More than any other writer, Rosabeth Kanter has focused on how important this integrative role is for middle managers if they are to function effectively in their organizations. This approach, which she documented in her 1983 book, *The Change Masters*, contrasts the segmentalist with the integrative organization.[16]

Poor Lateral Teamwork

Kanter describes a segmentalist organization as one in which specialists in each function operate virtually entirely within their own departments. They seldom venture across boundaries to integrate with their peers in other functions. Kanter says that people in other departments can seem irrelevant to middle manager when the structure and culture of his organization has a segmentalist orientation.

In a segmentalist firm—as opposed to an integrative one—Kanter has observed that middle managers seldom cross boundaries to secure organizational support and funds. In fact, there is little cooperation and teamwork among units. Instead, segments work independently and are walled off from other units. At the top, management does not acknowledge the importance of collaboration and integration and, instead, assigns to departments only fragments of problems. As a result, middle managers suffer from myopia; that is, they commonly see only one aspect of a particular problem.

In this environment, Kanter suggests, middle managers are more likely to guard their own turf, mend their own fences, and concentrate on pleasing their boss than to assist other people outside their own box on the organization chart. She found that although this behavior sometimes takes the form of direct conflict, more frequently it is passive, in the form of noncontact and noncommunication.

In contrast to the closed nature of the segmentalist firm, in the integrative firm Kanter noted that management assigns problems to "supraunits," such as task forces with middle managers from several departments. This cross-functional representation fosters a broader perspective that enables the team to consider the whole issue before developing a plan of action. These supraunits might take the form of a cross-functional team, a task force, or a project center. Kanter suggests that adaptive organizations have many integrative mechanisms encouraging middle managers to work together across boundaries, to share information, and to act on new knowledge gained from being able to have a broad perspective.

A Neglected Second Dimension?

By contrast, in the segmentalist firm—or what we like to call the up-down organization—middle managers function primarily through vertical channels, and not horizontally across departments. In the up-down organization, our experience is that middle managers operate in a vertical dimension, through vertical channels, not in a horizontal, or lateral, dimension.

One of the intentions of our research was to find out whether the inability of middle managers to function in a lateral dimension was contributing to their ineffectiveness and frustration. As middle managers face greater complexity today than in the past (as we noted in Chap. 1), a feeling of isolation could limit their effectiveness.

More than a decade ago, Jay Galbraith suggested that managers of large organizations were frequently faced with making decisions without proper information.[17] The complexity of their firm's operations limited the ability of managers to obtain the information they needed in a timely fashion. In his study of this problem, Galbraith spent a great deal of time examining the organizational structure and processes at Boeing. Clearly, Boeing is an example of a company managing a highly complex, technically demanding development and manufacturing process. Galbraith concluded that one choice managements have for building the capacity of their companies to process information and make effective decisions is to create lateral, cross-functional channels. (We discuss this concept in greater detail as the lateral dimension of the balanced organization in Chap. 5.)

At Boeing, Galbraith saw that it was simply impossible for middle managers to refer every problem up to senior management. Instead, middle managers solved problems at their own level, sharing information and working together with their peers in other departments.

To sum up, in organizations today we suspected that two factors were affecting middle managers and contributing to their ineffectiveness and discontent:

1. Career plateauing at the midlife stage, and
2. Poor lateral teamwork at their level.

A New Reality

We wanted to determine if these individual and organizational factors were giving middle managers the feeling that they were walled off from their peers in other parts of their organization. We speculated that the response of organizations to the New Competitive Reality had contributed to the sense of ineffectiveness and frustration we expected to document among middle managers.

We thought that the increased pressures resulting from changes in the competitive environment had exposed deficiencies in the structure and process of many organizations. These problems had not been evident in prior decades when the ranks of middle managers were expanding, spurred by rising profits and a less difficult competitive climate than is the case today.

By this time, we had developed a mental "map" of the world of middle managers, which is presented in Fig. 2.2. We can pull together and describe its various elements from what we have covered up to this point.

The "map" presented in Fig. 2.2 represents a chain, beginning with changes in the external environment, which we have described as the New Competitive Reality. Our view was that shifting trends in the external environment, such as deregulation, global competition, and pressure for short-term results create changes in the internal environment as organizations attempt to adapt to the New Competitive Reality.

Internally, we perceived that middle managers were functioning in a changed world with new requirements, resulting from *delegation of decision making; the growing complexity of cross-functional coordination; shorter time frames; increased reliance on data-based, not people-based, information systems; and organizational downsizing.*

Next, we thought that there were *individual factors*, related to career plateauing at midlife, and *organizational factors*, concerned with inadequate lateral teamwork, that resulted in the organizational outcome we were calling *a gap in the middle.*

Our experience in consulting with a variety of firms led us to suspect that changes in the external environment and the resulting attempts to adapt inside organizations had altered the world of middle managers. As a consequence, the findings of past studies might no longer be relevant.

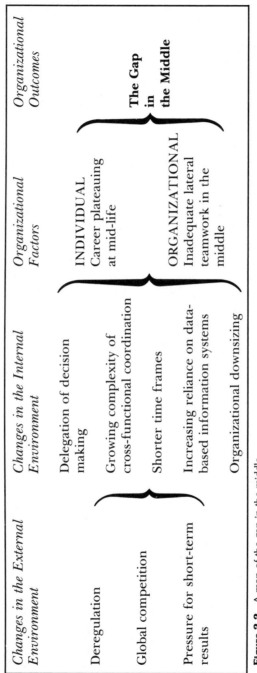

Changes in the External Environment	Changes in the Internal Environment	Organizational Factors	Organizational Outcomes
Deregulation	Delegation of decision making	INDIVIDUAL Career plateauing at mid-life	The Gap in the Middle
Global competition	Growing complexity of cross-functional coordination		
Pressure for short-term results	Shorter time frames	ORGANIZATIONAL Inadequate lateral teamwork in the middle	
	Increasing reliance on data-based information systems		
	Organizational downsizing		

Figure 2.2. A map of the gap in the middle.

Seeking Current Data: A Survey of Three Firms

Together with the limitations of the past research that we have mentioned, it was clear that we needed to develop current data to test our fundamental questions:

1. Is there a gap today at the middle-manager level in different types of organizations?

2. If a gap does exist, what are its principal causes?

To address these questions, we decided to conduct a formal, quantitative study to get the hard data we needed to test our views. In this section, we describe the survey we developed and the selection of three different organizations as sites. In the next chapter we discuss the results of these surveys and what we learned from them about the gap and its causes.

Our next steps were to develop a survey for collecting data and to select appropriate sites for conducting our survey. In the development of the survey, our aim was to go beyond the type of questions researchers usually incorporate in a quality-of-work-life survey in order to cover a wider range of business issues and organizational practices.

Our intention was to measure the views of people at all levels of an organization concerning a diverse range of issues, which we grouped under the following topics:

- Mission and strategic organizational objectives;
- Current competitive position of the organization;
- Communication, including cross-functional information exchange;
- Cooperation and teamwork;
- Delegation and decision making;
- People development, including training and career development;
- Managerial perspective;
- Risk taking;
- Problem solving;
- Action orientation;
- Management of change and growth, if applicable; and
- Management of reorganization and restructuring, if applicable.

(For a listing of sample questions contained in the survey, see the appendix at the back of the book.)

This extensive range of topics reflected our intent to measure the responses of middle managers, in comparison with people at other levels, across a broad spectrum of issues related to individuals as well as to organizational norms and practices. We wanted to understand the extent of the gap, if it did exist, as well as consider a number of issues that might suggest possible causes.

We were realistic enough to know that we would not be able to find answers beyond any doubt to our two key questions. At the same time, we selected three decidedly different organizations so that we would get a balanced as well as a broad view of what it was like to be a middle manager in today's competitive environment.

The three firms were characterized by differences across the spectrum of business strategy, competitive environment, market position, function, size, rate of growth, structure, formality, employment trend, average age of employees, years of service, and degree of technology. This diversity can be seen in Fig. 2.3, a summary description of these firms—which we called Matco, Salesco and Techco.[18]

Matco: On an Even Keel

The first organization in which we conducted our survey was Matco. This organization performs an internal service function coordinating the flow of materials—purchasing, scheduling, inventory control, and distribution—for a large manufacturing firm. In recent years, Matco's growth has plateaued, and employment has remained unchanged. The firm had, however, undertaken a major reorganization, which had begun a year before we conducted our survey, and the people in the organization were just beginning to become accustomed to the new structure.

Although the reorganization was extensive and resulted in new job titles for many people in the firm, no layoffs were involved and none were anticipated at the time of the survey. Matco is a single-career organization, in the sense that most employees came to work there as their first job out of school and stayed for their entire career. At the time of our study the average age of the people at Matco was 40, and they had been in the firm for an average of 17 years.

The culture of this organization reflects the steady pace of the work. Because Matco performs a service function for other departments in the corporation, in a sense it is removed from the immediate action of the

	MATCO	SALESCO	TECHCO
Business strategy	Upgrade quality and responsiveness of services	Maintain volume leadership through pricing and advertising	Aggressive volume leadership based on selling superiority
Competitive environment	Captive internal market, but a demanding one	Very competitive, new entrants taking share aggressively	Strong competition
Market position	Sole supplier of services	Still No. 1, but lead narrowing	Newly No. 1, lead growing
Function/product	Materials coordination	Consumer durable	Automated machinery
Sales volume	NA, static growth	Over $1 billion	$250 million
Structure	Formal hierarchy, 9 levels	Formal hierarchy, 9 levels	Informal hierarchy, 6 levels
Number of people	750	3,000	600
Employment trend	Static	Declining	Rising rapidly
Average age of people	40	40	28
Average years of service	17	18	2

Figure 2.3. A summary description of the three firms surveyed.

marketplace. People are conservative and, because of their long years of service, accustomed to a set routine. Bill Webb, the head of Matco, is a well-regarded old hand who was later promoted to a senior position at the top levels in the corporation. He is an excellent speaker, thoughtful, and even considered by some to be an intellectual.

Salesco: Still Number 1, But Slipping

The next organization we have called Salesco, reflecting the nature of its sales-oriented function. Salesco is a division of a major manufacturer of consumer durables. Although it has a proud history stretching back 75 years and is still the leader in its field, Salesco's market share has been declining steadily in the face of inroads from Japanese and, to a lesser extent, American competitors. The company had been through an extensive restructuring, which involved a reduction in staff from voluntary retirements, reassignments, and attrition.

In addition to the downsizing aspect of this restructuring, Salesco had been involved in an extensive reappraisal of its competitive position, which led to a major effort to reformulate its mission and to define and promulgate new goals and objectives. The new thrust was directed toward reducing the length of the new-product cycle, improving product quality, and reversing the decline in market share.

The release of monthly sales results and customer product-quality ratings is the focal point for nearly all Salesco's activities. The message has been unmistakable: "We must turn the slide around and regain the market share we have lost." The senior managers at Salesco have been intent on getting people to understand that the competitive world has changed, making a new sense of urgency vital.

The culture at Salesco reflects the up-down orientation of this organization where the protocol is very formal. Virtually everything is communicated up and down the hierarchy through formal, vertical channels. Senior managers are frequently addressed and referred to as "Mr. Wilson" or "Mr. Swift." Visits by the top brass to the field are carefully staged productions, with much advance preparation, a fleet of limousines, and tightly organized schedules. Rank and a person's position in the hierarchy are important and visible. In introducing themselves, people would immediately indicate their level: "I'm a 6," or "I'm a 4."

John Wilson, the general manager of Salesco, is a brusque, no-nonsense, blunt man in his sixties and in the last assignment of a long, successful career. He is competitive and openly concerned with protecting Salesco's turf vis-à-vis other departments in the corporation. Although he clearly intimidates some of the members of his staff, he has surrounded himself with a number of people who are not hesitant to speak up when they think their boss is off track.

As at Matco, the majority of the people at Salesco have spent virtually their entire careers in the Salesco organization. At the time of our study the average age was also 40, and the length of time in the organization was 18 years. It is customary for people to remain in one functional specialty for their entire time in the company. In turn, the focus of training is directed toward keeping technical skills up to date in a long-established area of specialization.

Techco: High Tech and Growing Like a Weed

When we turned our attention to the third organization, Techco, we entered a different world. In direct contrast to mature, established firms like Matco and Salesco, Techco is an upstart. The company is a joint venture of a major American corporation and an international partner. It had taken Techco only four years to achieve annual sales of $250 million and to become the leader in its high-tech field. Whereas the dominant disciplines at Salesco are sales and finance, at Techco they are engineering and R&D. Working at Techco was like being at Apple Compuer or Sun Microsystems in the early days.

The pace at Techco is fast-moving, and the atmosphere is youthful and informal. On Fridays, for example, employees are urged to dress informally with the result that a contest seems to develop every week to see who can wear the wildest shirt. At the time of our study the average age of the people at Techco was 28, more than 10 years less than that at the other firms.

Rank is seemingly unimportant at Techco. The open configuration of the offices reflects the informality and lack of pretension. Only a few of the top officers had closed offices, and in the new building that was under construction, the plans called for everyone to have an open office.

Lars Nelson, the head of the Techco organization, is in his fifties, two to three decades older than most of the members of his organization. He is a people-oriented manager who emphasizes open communication throughout the company. At the conclusion of frequent all-company meetings, he holds impromptu question-and-answer sessions where people ask him a wide range of questions and openly express their concerns.

Downsizing and staff reductions were clearly not problems for middle managers at Techco. Instead, Techco was expanding rapidly in an effort to keep up with incoming business. Even though Techco had established a leadership position, competition in its markets remained keen. A great deal of the organization's attention is directed to introducing new products that are in the vanguard of technology. At the time of our survey, Techco was experiencing difficulties in reducing the length of the new-product cycle, a critical aspect in the firm's efforts to continue to grow rapidly and in its goal to dominate the industry.

These three sites were clearly different across many dimensions. On the one hand, for example, Salesco had experienced the pressures of downsizing and losing market share; Techco, on the other hand, was expanding rapidly and was experiencing growing pains. Together with Matco, which was running on an even keel, these three firms provided us with a chance to test our questions about middle managers in a variety of circumstances.

When all the surveys were completed, we had information from 2600 people at all job levels in these three firms, including 600 middle managers. On balance, the results confirmed what our conversations with middle managers had led us to expect. At the same time, there were also a few surprises that proved to be vital to us when we began to develop action steps for senior and middle managers to follow in order to close the gap in the middle. These specific action steps are outlined in Part 3, "Leading from the Middle."

In the next chapter, you will see that the conventional wisdom of "hear no gap, see no gap" in the middle is no longer valid. As we had expected, the world of middle managers had changed in the face of the New Competitive Reality.

Endnotes

1. Chris Argyris, *Personality and Organization*, New York: Harper & Row, 1957.
2. These two studies are C. I. Hulin and P. C. Smith, "A Linear Model of Job Satisfaction," *Journal of Applied Psychology*, 1965, Vol. 49, No. 3, pp. 209–216 and E. F. Adams, D. R. Laker, and C. I. Hulin, "An Investigation of the Influence of Job Level and Functional Specialty on Job Attitudes and Perceptions," *Journal of Applied Psychology*, 1977, Vol. 62, No. pp. 335–343.
3. D. T. Hall, B. Schneider, and H. Nygren, "Personal Factors in Organizational Identification," *Administrative Science Quarterly*, 1970, Vol. 15, pp. 176–190.
4. Jeffrey Pfeffer, "Organizational Demography: Implications for Management," *California Management Review*, 1985, Vol. 28, No. 2, pp. 67–82. In our experience, surprisingly few organizational researchers pay attention to this point. Pfeffer is a welcome exception.

5. Paul Lawrence mentioned this point during a seminar at the Boston University School of Management on April 7, 1987. The title of Lawrence's talk was "Differentiation and Integration Revisited." This reference is to the pioneering work by Lawrence and Jay Lorsch published by Harvard Business School Press in 1967 entitled *Organization and the Environment*.

6. Barry Oshry has written several very useful articles on the subject of "middles" including *Middle Power* in 1980 and *Middles of the World, Integrate!* in 1982. Both are published by his firm, Power & Systems Training, Inc., P. O. Box 388, Prudential Station, Boston, MA 02199.

7. Gail Sheehy, *Passages: Predictable Crises of Adult Life*, New York: Bantam Books, 1977.

8. F. J. Smith, K. D. Scott, and C. I. Hulin, "Trends in Job-Related Attitudes of Managerial and Professional Employees," *Academy of Management Journal*, 1977, Vol. 20, No. 3, 454–460.

9. M. Sheldon, "Investments and Involvements as Mechanisms in Producing Commitment to the Organization," *Administrative Science Quarterly*, 1971, pp. 143–150.

10. G. R. Salancik, "Commitment and Control of Organizational Behavior and Belief," in B. Staw and G. R. Salancik, *New Directions in Organizational Behavior*, Chicago: St. Clair Press, 1978.

11. Harry Levinson, "On Being a Middle-Aged Manager," *Harvard Business Review*, July/August 1969, pp. 51–60.

12. Daniel Levinson and Associates, *The Seasons of a Man's Life*, New York: Ballantine Books, 1978.

13. D. T. Hall, *Careers in Organizations*, Santa Monica, CA: Goodyear Publishing Company, 1976, and E. Schein, *Career Dynamics*, Reading, MA: Addison-Wesley, 1978.

14. Judith Bardwick, *The Plateauing Trap*, New York: AMACOM, 1986. This is a thorough and thoughtful study of the impact of changing social and economic factors on the professional and personal lives of managers.

15. See especially Barry Oshry's *Middle Power*, which he published in 1980.

16. Rosabeth Moss Kanter, *The Change Masters*, New York: Simon and Schuster, 1983.

17. Jay Galbraith, *Organizational Design*, Reading, MA: Addison-Wesley, 1977. This study is a classic that we revisit frequently for insights in our work in organizations.

18. As we noted in the Preface, for reasons of confidentiality we have chosen to use fictitious names for the organizations in this study and the people in them.

3

For Middle Managers, The Gap Is Real

From the study, we found some things we expected to find, and some we didn't. To begin with, the study confirmed what we had expected to find about the existence of a gap in the middle: *Middle managers are discontented and frustrated. For middle managers, the gap is real.*

Indeed, the existence of a gap was inescapable—it was present across a broad range of issues and practices. The gap was clear, not just for specific *individual* concerns such as job satisfaction or promotion, but also for the full range of business issues and *systemwide* organizational practices we had measured.

The analysis identified 11 significant factors from this data.[1] We found that gaps were evident at the middle-management level for the six factors listed below. (For each factor, we have included comments from middle managers to illustrate these points.)

1. Senior management's concern for employees:

   "Decisions are made in this company without asking the people who will have to live with them."

   "People who get ahead in this company aren't those who are willing to stick their necks out."

   "Sometimes I think that our management cares more about money and machines than people."

2. Communication of and commitment to the firm's mission:

   "Our mission statement won't really turn people on or off. It will have no effect at all."

"I am not contributing much personally to the success of our mission."

3. Adequacy of long-term planning:

"People are rewarded for short-term results in spite of long-term shortfalls."

"Our productivity suffers from a lack of organization and planning."

"Often, we look for a quick fix rather than a long-term solution to problems."

4. Individual autonomy:

"I have to check with lots of people before I can do anything new in this company."

"Everything here has to be handled through channels."

"People at my level (middle managers) don't have enough authority to do their jobs well."

5. Management of change/reorganization:

"The level of decision making isn't moving down."

Speaking of the recent reorganization, a middle manager told us: "This, too, will pass."

6. Customer satisfaction:

"We still aren't doing a satisfactory job of satisfying the customer."

"We are too late with new products, we are a follower—not a leader."

"Our products don't have a clear identity in the market."

As these factors indicate, *we found patterns unlike those in the past studies that we described in the previous chapter.*[2] Instead of the consistently more favorable response for each successively higher level in the organization, we found a break in the progression at the middle-manager level. The studies we reviewed in Chap. 2 suggested that we would find a pattern like that in the left chart in Fig. 3.1; in contrast, what we actually found is shown in the right chart. The results from our study (Fig. 3.1, on the right) indicate that middle managers (level 4) are less positive than those above them at level 5. Moreover, contradicting the conventional wisdom drawn from past studies, middle managers were less positive than those just below them in the organization at level 3.

Further, the analysis showed that middle managers are also less positive than those immediately above and below them—to a somewhat less significant extent—for three additional factors:

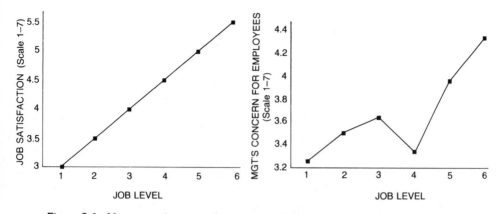

Figure 3.1. Management's concern for employees (Middle managers are level 4.)

7. Career development:

"I don't get the job assignments I need to help me develop my career."

"We need to have more management-development training to help us broaden our skills."

8. Teamwork with people in other departments:

"People in other departments often stand in the way of what we're trying to accomplish in my area."

"There is a lot of tension and rivalry between departments in this company."

9. Communication from senior management:

"They don't really keep us well informed about what's going on and the changes they're making."

"A lot of times, the information just doesn't seem to filter down to our level. There seems to be a block just above us."

"The 5s (the level above middle managers) are on a lot of key committees and teams that we aren't. At those meetings, they can tap into the network and find out what's going on . . .who is doing well and who screwed up."

Figure 3.2 illustrates this less strong, but nevertheless apparent, evidence of a gap.

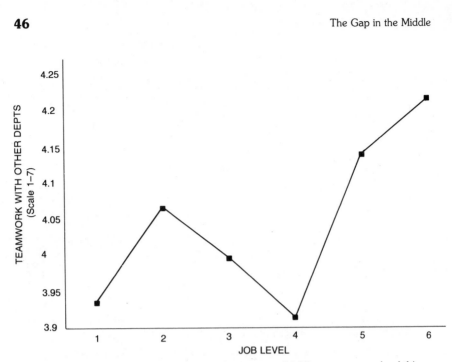

Figure 3.2. Teamwork with people in other departments. (Middle managers are level 4.)

This pattern suggests a wider gap, with less positive responses at both levels 3 and 4. Again, there is a clear break in the trend of steadily more favorable responses found in past studies. Finally, only in the case of two of the 11 factors did our findings reflect the conventional wisdom described in Chap. 2. Gaps were *not* evident for the following:

10. Support from the supervisors:

    "My boss encourages me to find better ways to do my job."

    "My supervisor gives me the freedom to make changes in the way I do my work."

11. Teamwork within their own work groups:

    "The people in my group work well together as a team."

    "My team comes up with new ideas which help us to work better."

Figure 3.3 illustrates this pattern of step-by-step increases in the level of response from one level to the next.

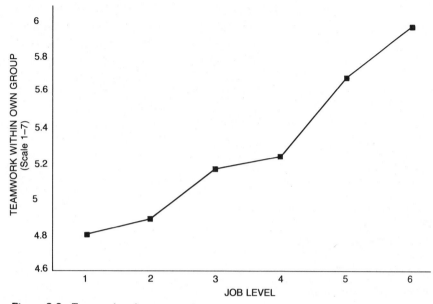

Figure 3.3. Teamwork within own work group. (Middle managers are level 4.)

The Gap Is Both Vertical and Horizontal

The contrasting trends reflected in the last two figures (3.2 and 3.3) indicate that although middle managers feel that teamwork is good within their own departments, they complained of tension and rivalries with middle managers in other departments. Although we found that middle managers are positive about the relationships with their immediate boss and with the other people in their group, they feel isolated and, in fact, walled off (1) *vertically* from management above them (e.g., senior management's concern for employees and communication from senior management), and (2) *horizontally* from their peers in other departments in their firm (e.g., teamwork with people in other departments).

In Chaps. 4 and 5, we return to this point and elaborate on the importance to middle managers of both vertical and horizontal dimensions. *This study suggests that middle managers are isolated behind walls that need to be torn down if they are to be effective in meeting the challenges they face today.*

In summary, this analysis shows that for 9 of the 11 factors there was clear evidence of a gap at the middle-manager level. Middle managers were less positive than those above and below them across a wide range of both individual and organizational issues.

Also, we should note that in looking at the separate analyses of the responses from each of the three organizations, we found that there is actually not much evidence of a gap at Matco (which we will discuss later in this chapter) while the gap is unmistakable at Salesco and Techco. In the next section, when we look at the possible causes for middle managers' feelings of discontent and isolation, this distinction will be especially useful.

Survey Data Sheds New Light on Causes

Plateauing Discarded

As we reviewed the responses from people at Salesco, we could see that the middle managers who were most pessimistic were those in the middle of their careers. Here, once again, was evidence of Daniel Levinson's notion of a midlife transition. As these middle managers reached their forties, it was becoming apparent to them that their careers had plateaued.

At Salesco, it is not surprising that middle managers felt plateaued. In addition to the pyramid effect, the chances for promotion were limited because the overall business was shrinking, and the organization was being downsized. The following comment was typical of many we heard:

> Now that we aren't growing anymore, my chances for promotion really aren't that good any longer.

Also, the people who received the best assignments as a result of the recent reorganization were a decidedly younger group than had occupied positions of such importance in the past. Some of Salesco's middle managers were beginning to feel that their chances for promotion were slipping away:

> They made a definite shift in the type of people they promoted at the time of the reorganization. They are much younger and more aggressive than the type of people they have promoted before. There's a real message for people like me that seniority and experience aren't that important any more.

Consequently, it is understandable that the responses to the survey from the middle-aged, middle-manager group would reflect these disappointments about the future of their careers. Our findings confirmed the distinctions that Gerry Salancik had suggested (see Chap. 2) on the basis of age. On the one hand, we found that the more positive middle managers were in two age groups:

1. Younger people who still had promotions ahead of them, and

2. Older managers who had accepted the likelihood that they would no longer be promoted.

On the other hand, those with negative views of their future were between these two groups in age. For these middle-aged managers, the level of frustration was high as they were beginning to understand that their chances for another promotion were much smaller than they had previously thought.

At the other end of the spectrum, when we shifted our attention to Techco, we expected to see a different picture. Techco was a young organization where the average age was in the late twenties. In the entire 600-person organization, there were only a handful of individuals who were over 40. Hardly anyone at Techco was old enough to be having a "midlife crisis," to use the expression Gail Sheehy made famous. Also, the firm was growing so rapidly that the chances of promotion were increasing as the company grew. As a result, the pyramid effect was not an issue at Techco.

As a result, if midcareer plateauing was indeed the clear-cut cause of the discontent among middle managers, we would not have expected to find a gap at Techco. However, we were surprised at what we found. In fact, on the contrary, at Techco the gap was even more pronounced than at Salesco.

Clearly, downsizing and the merge and purge process were not the only causes of frustration among middle managers. Although midcareer plateauing may be related to the gap in the middle in some firms, it did not account for the gap in others.

So, we set aside career plateauing as a generalized cause of the gap. We turned to the second potential cause we had formulated at the outset, thinking it might lead us to a more generalized, or universal, cause of the gap.

Poor Lateral Teamwork Confirmed

Our study indicated that at both Techco and Salesco where the evidence of a gap was clear, middle managers had a far less positive view than those above and below them of the cooperation and teamwork with their peers in other departments. (See Fig. 3.2.)

The survey responses showed that middle managers felt an unusually high degree of tension and rivalry with people in other functional areas. Turf battles across departmental boundaries were common among middle managers. In many instances, they looked at people in other departments as competitors rather than partners

> We don't really get along with Purchasing. They have their agenda, and we have ours.

In comparison with people at other levels, middle managers were less positive about the willingness of people in other departments to provide them with the information and cooperation they needed to perform their own assignments. In short, at the middle-management level, the teamwork across functions is much less effective than at other levels.

This issue is important since middle managers said they need a lot of cooperation from their peers in other departments. Yet, they also showed that they have the hardest time getting the cooperation they require to do their jobs.

Both Salesco and Techco are up-down organizations, that is, the communication flow is up and down the hierarchy. At the middle-management level, the focus of attention is vertical, not lateral. Lateral coordination and integration among functions take place at the senior-management level in these firms, not at the middle-management level.

At Salesco, middle managers were being given more responsibility as the firm attempted to adjust to rapid change and a market that appeared increasingly unpredictable. Salesco was trying to get "closer to the customer." Senior managers were "pushing decisions down" to middle managers, who are "closer to the action." In the past, middle managers had passed too many decisions up the ladder, and the vertical channels were now clogged.

However, for the middle managers at Salesco to take on this added decision making effectively, they needed information and cooperation from other departments. Cross-functional coordination is required at the middle-management level, not just at the top as before. Yet, the survey showed that middle managers felt teamwork with other departments was poor. As we shared the results of the survey with middle managers at Salesco, many people told us of specific instances of turf battles with other departments. They said that people in other areas of the company often acted more like competitors than collaborators working toward the same goal.

> Your results show that we don't get along with people in Operations. That is right-on. We've got to get our problems out on the table. We've got to try again to resolve our differences.

In addition to tracking their share of the overall consumer market, they also kept figures showing the standing of their division in relation to the other divisions in the company. They have the largest share within the corporation, and they wanted the other divisions to know it.

At Techco, the problem concerning coordination at the middle-manager level was different—an inability to introduce new products rapidly and smoothly. Though the firm had achieved a leadership position in the market in only four years, the last several new-product introductions had not gone smoothly. Coordination across departments had been ineffectual, and schedules had slipped. Lars Nelson, the president, commented:

> Getting new products introduced on time is our biggest problem at Techco. If we don't resolve this problem, we'll lose our competitive position in no time.

The survey showed that middle managers at Techco were also frustrated by poor teamwork and a lack of cooperation from other departments. Again, like our experience at Salesco, when we reviewed the survey results with middle managers in individual departments, they confirmed that teamwork across functions was poor. In fact, they went a step further and identified specific departments where collaboration was ineffective. They indicated that teamwork was especially ineffective when the pressure was on not to fall behind schedule for the introduction of a new product.

Although their immediate circumstances were different, it became apparent at both Salesco and Techco that the ability of the middle managers to do their jobs requires that they be able to function laterally. They need information and cooperation from middle managers in other departments.

Middle managers in these firms were being asked to take on more responsibility. In many instances, senior managers were delegating more operating decisions to the middle-management levels, and this process was revealing deficiencies in their organization's structures and procedures that had not been apparent before.

The Impact of Rapid Change

Both Salesco and Techco face a rapidly changing external environment as a result of deregulation, increased global competition, and the necessity

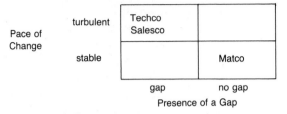

Figure 3.4. Relationship between the pace of change and the gap in the middle.

of producing good financial results every quarter. Reflecting these changes, middle managers are faced with tasks and challenges that require them to be able to function effectively in a lateral dimension.

While the external environment was stable at Matco, it had clearly become a great deal more complex and turbulent at both Salesco and Techco. Figure 3.4 illustrates the relationship between the pace of change in the environment and the presence of a gap in the middle.

Whether the pressures are those associated with a declining market share and downsizing as at Salesco or are related to rapid growth and growing pains as at Techco, the impact of the rapid pace of change is the most disruptive for people at the middle-manager level.

The middle managers are the people feeling the most heat. At the companies we studied they were being asked to do more, but often allowances had not been made for their changed responsibilities. For middle managers to function effectively, the structure and procedures of their firms need to have a lateral orientation as well as a vertical one. The need to integrate across departments at the middle-management level as well as at the top is clear.

This discussion of the causes of the gap at the middle-manager level suggests that in some instances the discontent may be related to a sense of being walled in by a dead-end career. However, a more universal cause, which applies to even those firms with expanding career opportunities, lies in inadequate structural arrangements and procedures that were not apparent during the period from 1950 to 1975 when the ranks of middle managers were growing. Now that the growth is over, the cracks are showing.

Other Distinctions from the Survey

In addition, the distinctions among the three organizations also permitted us to explore several other relationships. For instance in the case of the trend of employment, the pattern was like that in the previous figure. The level of employment is stable at Matco where a gap is not evident. Yet, as shown in Fig. 3.5, where major changes in employment have taken

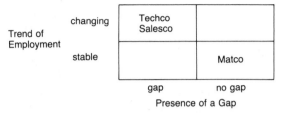

Figure 3.5. Relationship between the trend of employment and the presence of a gap in the middle.

place (at Techco employment was increasing rapidly while at Salesco there had been reductions in force), a gap was evident.

At the same time, for several other dimensions there does not appear to be a consistent relationship with the existence of a gap. For instance, the degree of formality in an organization's hierarchy does not appear related to the presence of a gap, as is illustrated in Fig. 3.6. At Salesco, the hierarchy is very formal, and distinctions associated with different levels are apparent. On the other hand, the Techco organization is informal, and there is little evidence of "rank."

Similarly, the existence of a gap appears to be unrelated to whether people are positive or negative in their overall view of their organization. Among the middle managers across a full range of factors, those at Techco were the most positive of the three firms, followed by those at Matco while middle managers at Salesco were the least positive. This is illustrated in Fig. 3.7.

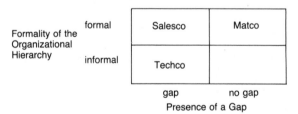

Figure 3.6. The relationship between organizational formality and the presence of a gap in the middle.

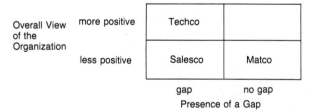

Figure 3.7. The relationship between the view of the organization and the presence of a gap in the middle.

Finally, the gap does not appear to be related to the age of people in the organization nor to their length of service. Gaps were present both at Techco where the average age was 28 and length of service two years and, at the opposite end of the spectrum, at Salesco where the average age was much older at 40 and the length of service considerably longer at 18 years.

In summary, this study suggests that the existence of a gap may be related to certain elements and not to others.

The existence of a gap may be related to:

1. Poor lateral teamwork in the middle;

2. A feeling of isolation from senior management;

3. An unstable, turbulent external environment; and

4. Major shifts in the level of employment in the organization—whether rising or declining.

The existence of a gap may not be related to:

1. Formality of an organization's hierarchy;

2. The middle manager's degree of positiveness about the organization;

3. Average age of people in the firm; and

4. Length of service.

The New Reality Revised

Our findings meant that we needed to revise our original map of the gap, set out in Fig. 2.2 in Chap. 2. Specifically, now we knew that the causes of the gap were more related to organizational factors, such as vertical and lateral processes, than to individual factors, such as plateauing in mid-career.

The organizational issues raised in the analysis suggested that short-comings existed in both vertical and horizontal dimensions. So, we revised the original map; our new map is shown in Fig. 3.8.

This figure suggests why a gap was not apparent at Matco. To begin with, Bill Webb and his senior staff worked hard to communicate down through all levels of the organization. The survey data from Matco indicated that this effort had been successful: There was no evidence of a gap at the middle-management level related to communication from senior management. At Matco, this factor was not contributing to a gap.

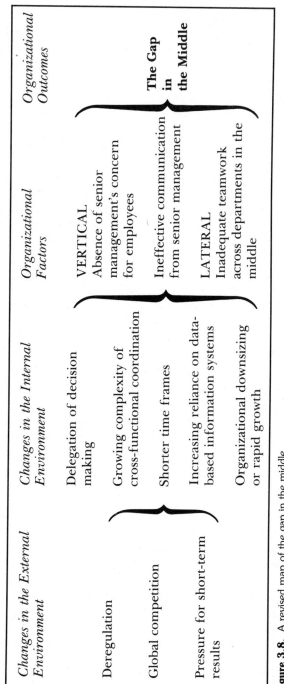

Figure 3.8. A revised map of the gap in the middle.

The second explanation is that Matco is insulated from changes in the environment. Matco had been affected—far less than Salesco and Techco—by deregulation, global competition, and financial pressures in the external environment. As we indicated, Matco serves a captive market. It is a sole-source supplier, so its customer does not have the option of going elsewhere. Also, because Matco's management has a good record of controlling costs, people at Matco are not under as severe pressure to improve their results.

Turn to the segment of the figure labeled "changes in the internal environment." At Matco, there has not been any downsizing, nor has there been any appreciable shortening in time frames. Although there has been greater reliance on data-based information systems, they were introduced gradually and initially at lower levels in the organization. Also, the growing complexity of cross-functional coordination tends to help Matco's position in relation to other departments. Because Matco provides a service function, supporting such departments as engineering and production, growing complexity led these departments to rely more and more on Matco to support their work.

Middle Managers in the New Reality

Middle managers had a less difficult time in earlier decades when American firms had their home market to themselves, and the pressure from world competitors was less demanding. Today, however, the New Competitive Reality has uncovered and brought to the surface weaknesses in organizational structure and processes at the middle-management level. The result is a gap among middle managers that is holding back American business firms in their efforts to become fully competitive in world markets.

In effect, middle managers have become isolated because of clogged vertical channels and inadequate lateral ones. Being a middle manager in many of today's organizations is like being walled in, a feeling of being isolated both vertically and laterally.

Before turning to a review of what we believe needs to be done by both senior and middle managers to remove the walls that are isolating middle managers, we want to take a more in-depth look at what it is like to be a middle manager today in a variety of different types of organizations. In order to elaborate on the results of our survey, we spoke with a number of middle managers in these three firms as well as in other companies. We wanted to take a closer look at life inside the walls.

Endnotes

1. A more detailed description of the data and the statistical analysis from this study is contained in the following unpublished doctoral dissertation by Leonard W. Johnson: *Identifying and Closing the Gap in the Middle of Organizations*, Boston University School of Management, 1989. A copy can be obtained from University Microfilm in Ann Arbor, Michigan.

2. Since only three firms were involved in this study, we recognize that our conclusions need additional testing. We offer them here for the reader to compare with his or her own experience.

PART 2
Taking the Heat in the Middle

4
Behind the Walls of the Up-Down Company

What our study confirmed is that the heightened *external* pressures resulting from what we call the New Competitive Reality are having the most pronounced *internal* impact in organizations at the middle-management level. Middle managers are taking the heat.

The financial pressures reflected in the merge and purge syndrome as well as the growing complexities of managing worldwide operations, of producing products of world-class quality, of introducing products more rapidly than world competitors—these pressures are especially acute for middle managers. In the up-down firm these competitive forces have exposed weaknesses in managerial practices and in the structural arrangements of American corporations, which had been masked in a less competitive world.

Managing Vertically: Still Following Moses

We know from the Bible that Moses established one of the first up-down organizations based on divine advice.

> Choose able men from all the people... and place such men over the people as rulers of thousands, of hundreds, of fifties, and of tens. And let them judge the people at all times; every great matter they shall bring to you, but any small matter they shall decide themselves....
>
> Exodus 18: 21–22

For centuries, we have built on this set of principles for organizing and managing. The predominant dimension in organizations is still vertical. We think that many organizations have taken these principles too far and that, by themselves, they are no longer appropriate.

The vertical chain of command still represents the heart of the structure and processes of most American companies. Most firms have an up-down orientation; that is, information goes up the chain to the top; direction, evaluation, and rewards come back down. Middle managers are responsible for their own, specialized units, and their focus is on their particular piece of the organizational puzzle.

Our discussions with middle managers confirmed what the results of our study had indicated—that problems resulting from an organization's structure and practices are a key cause of the gap. Building on the factors related to the gap highlighted in the previous chapter, we now discuss how the basic aspects of managerial practices and of functional structure in an up-down organization affect middle managers.

To begin with, three of the factors set out at the beginning of Chap. 3 are related to organizational practices for vertical communication:

- Senior management's concern for employees (Factor #1),

- Communication of and commitment to the firm's mission (Factor #2), and

- Communication from senior management (Factor #9).

As we discussed the findings of the study with middle managers, it became apparent that these issues of communication result from:

1. The mixed messages and contradictions that middle managers receive from their bosses;

2. Delegation and the lack of information that accompanied the delegation of operational decisions to middle managers; and

3. The overreliance on vertical channels by everyone in the up-down company.

Up-Down Organizational Practices That Perpetuate the Gap, Round 1

Mixed Messages for Middle Managers

Many of the messages middle managers receive involve contradictions. From their perspective, they are being asked to make sense of many catch-22 directives:

- Manage for the long term *and* produce good short-term profits;
- Think strategically *and* be quick fixers;
- Cut costs *and* be empathetic toward their subordinates;
- Be lean *and* increase workers' commitment and loyalty to the firm;
- Improve controls *and* encourage risk taking and creativity;
- Cut corners *and* be ethical; and
- Be on top of their work *and* delegate.

For middle managers, these contradictions represent a mine field of potential problems. Their job requires that they do both, so it is clearly difficult to be 100 percent consistent. Middle managers are frustrated by being whipsawed as they try to respond to these conflicting messages that make them look inconsistent to their subordinates as well as uninformed about what is really going on.

Double Speak: Walking Like We Talk

In one large manufacturing organization, we often heard middle managers comment on the importance of being consistent:

> We all have to walk like we talk. Won't they ever understand that? I'm really tired of being jerked around all the time.

In this firm, an especially exasperating contradiction involved the new campaign to improve product quality. As a part of the new mission and strategy, senior management had set the goal of producing products that met world-class standards as a paramount part of the business plan to recapture lost market share.

Management devoted a great deal of attention to communicating the importance of this goal. They held a series of off-site meetings for all senior and middle managers to stress its significance of quality to the business plan. A quality "czar" was appointed at a senior level in the organization. The firm also spent large sums sending many of its middle managers to "quality college" for a week or more of specialized training. The moment of truth arrived at the time of the introduction of new models for the coming year. In this company, model changeover is "crunch time" when you find out what management really thinks is important. In this particular year, when the middle managers began to hold back production in order to ensure that the new models met high quality standards, the backtracking on this issue was swift and unmistakable. The message from the top couldn't have been clearer:

> We don't care what you boys do, we can't afford to miss any more production. That killed us last year. Just find a way to "muscle them through."

The middle managers felt they had been whipsawed by their senior management. Their credibility was compromised. They complained that this reversal made them look foolish in the eyes of their subordinates. They felt that it was essential for their actions to be consistent with their words. The middle managers in this company believed that it is important to "walk like we talk."

Delegation Without the Facts

Over the last several years, in response to the pressures of the New Competitive Reality enumerated earlier, senior managers at many American corporations have felt that they were being swamped with the increasing complexity of managing a global business. It became impossible for them to manage everything at the top. In many instances, they responded by opting to move decisions related to operations down to middle managers.

When senior managers attempt to move a decision to a lower level in their firm, new channels for sharing information need to be established. In many organizations, however, we found that senior managers balked at the idea of sharing more information.

Tracy Kidder was the first person to call our attention to the "mushroom theory of management." In his award-winning book, *The Soul of a New Machine*, about the development of a new computer by a team of engineers at Data General, he describes the management style of one of the managers as patterned after the mushroom theory of management: "put 'em in the dark, feed 'em shit, and watch 'em grow."[1]

Delegation without information is a nightmare for middle managers. One manager described his experience with delegation as follows:

> Management tells us that they want to move decisions down to our level. It's just lip service. The first time we made the decision about which outside supplier to use, our bosses reversed our decision, saying that we were unaware of a critical factor—there were provisions in the labor agreement with the unions which restricted our ability to outsource those parts. Why didn't they give us the full picture in the first place?

Incomplete delegation also occurs when management divides a problem and assigns part of it to one department, part to another, and so on. This process of divide and confuse often means that the problem solvers at the middle management level are seeing only a part of the problem and are acting on the basis of incomplete information. In many firms, it is common to regard the coordinating function as the sole domain of managers at the top.

Clogged Vertical Channels

Excessive reliance on vertical channels is common for middle managers in many organizations. This practice represents an important structural and procedural deficiency and accounts for much of the ineffectiveness of middle managers; it creates what Richard Pascale calls the "chimney effect."[2] Frequently, we found that middle managers regarded their peers in other departments not as collaborators but as competitors. Often, middle managers focused their efforts more on guarding their own turf than on tearing down the walls keeping people out.

One place where protecting one's turf is common is at Salesco. Although a great deal of attention is directed toward regaining share of the overall market, there is also another agenda—to do what is necessary to maintain Salesco's position *within* the firm as the largest division. For people at Salesco, it is vital that they retain their position at the top of the pecking order.

The way managers are evaluated and rewarded reinforces this myopic view. In our experience, people are rated on the basis of their performance in their "home" departments and not on how well they cooperate and collaborate with people in other departments. Again, the structure and procedures of the "up-down" firm do not acknowledge the importance of integration—lateral information sharing and teamwork—at the middle-manager level.

Next, before turning to this key aspect of organizational structure, there are three additional factors related to the gap that also involve organizational practices:

- Adequacy of long-range planning (Factor #3),
- Individual autonomy (Factor #4), and
- Management of change/reorganization (Factor #5).

Up-Down Organizational Practices That Perpetuate the Gap, Round 2

The Impact of Change and Reorganization

The reorganization and downsizing at Salesco had the biggest impact on the lives of the middle managers in the organization. Laying people off, changing structure, consolidating units—all typical aspects of downsizing—create disruption and upset established methods of operation. They require new patterns of interaction and new networks for middle managers. Old relationships and contacts often fade away. These changes may be for the better—but the cost of these disruptions for middle management is rarely taken into account.

Our experience suggests that it takes middle managers two to four years to settle down from a major reorganization. While stress is high and the pressures are great on everyone, it is the middle managers who must bear the burden of the change. Simultaneously, they are expected to keep the organization productive as well as prepare for the new order. One middle manager described this process in the following terms:

> During the reorganization, we are expected to do two jobs. One is to keep the company running, and the second is to get the procedures and everything ready for a smooth start-up of the new organization. Everyone has a new assignment and has to learn a new way of doing things. Management doesn't seem to appreciate that all these meetings take a great deal of time and effort. All the while, we are expected to keep doing our old jobs. There just aren't enough hours in the week to do it all.

Typically, it is middle managers who are the most affected by these efforts to become more competitive. For new programs such as quality improvement, getting close to the customer, and employee involvement, middle managers must learn a new approach to organizing and managing. They need to acquire a new vocabulary and new skills; some will be useful in the long run, others will not. Whether useful or not, middle managers have learned that there is always a risk that "this, too, will pass" as management moves on from one attempt at a quick fix to another. Indeed, we found that one of the most common terms in the vocabulary of middle managers is "the quick fix."

Inadequate Planning and the Quick Fix

Another factor from the study where there was evidence of a gap concerned middle managers views of the inadequacy of long-range planning in their organization. As we have indicated, many middle managers face the contradiction that they are expected to plan strategically *and* to be quick fixers.

The pressure on the senior management of American companies to manage for the short term is greater than that experienced by their counterparts in Europe and Japan. This pressure to produce favorable short-term results directly affects the jobs of middle-managers. Again, we found that the turbulence in the outside environment has its greatest impact inside the organization at the middle manager level.

Next, we shift our attention from deficiencies in organizational practices to problems with organizational structure that we found in the up-down firm.

Up-Down Organizational Structure Perpetuates the Gap

Lack of Teamwork in the Middle

Most up-down organizations that use a traditional, hierarchical structure give the senior managers at the top the responsibility for coordinating the activities of the different functional departments. Integration, then, is primarily the responsibility of top management and is often implemented through a series of cross-functional committees, patterned after the approach to integration that Alfred Sloan pioneered at General Motors in the 1920s.

Now that responsibility for many operational decisions is being delegated to people at the middle-management level, they need information not only from senior managers but also from people in other departments. For middle managers to be able to manage the responsibility for an increasing number of decisions concerning day-to-day operations, they need to be able to function in an integrating role. *Integration is necessary in the middle for operational decisions just as it is at the top for overall direction and strategic planning.*

As the results of our survey confirmed, however, in the up-down organization it is especially difficult for middle managers to get the information and cooperation they need. In these companies, the primary communication channels for middle managers are vertical, not lateral. The coordination process involves going up the ladder to the top in one department and then down the ladder in the other department. The structure does not recognize that delegation has expanded the location of the need for integration beyond those at the top to include managers in the middle ranks as well.

Middle-Manager Myopia: A Limited Perspective

The feeling of many middle managers that they are walled in and isolated reflects the segmentation that Rosabeth Kanter found in many American business firms (see Chap. 2).[3] People are promoted to the middle-management ranks on the basis of their competence in specialized roles.

The pattern of specialization we found at Salesco is common in other firms as well.

For example, at Apple Computer in 1985 a disagreement arose between Donna Dubinsky and Debi Coleman, two middle managers, over a proposed change in the system of distributing computers to dealers.[4] Dubinsky, a Harvard MBA, was in charge of distribution and resented what she considered intrusions into "her" territory by Coleman, a Stanford MBA, who was in charge of manufacturing for the new MacIntosh line. In addition to Dubinsky's desire to protect her own turf, her inability to see the problem from any perspective beyond that of her own specialty hampered the process of resolving the issue.

Increasingly, middle managers are rewarded for knowing a great deal about a specialized area. Middle managers often spend their entire careers in one area of the business. Their training is aimed at keeping their skills up to date in their area of specialization. As the world becomes more complex and the pace of information flow quickens, middle managers must concentrate on staying on top of their responsibilities. This is ironic because making sense of complexity and understanding information requires a broader perspective of areas beyond one's own area of expertise.

Middle managers are rewarded for being specialists in several ways. To begin with, they are referred to as "experts." This description has great prestige in our knowledge-based society. Second, on issues that touch on their field of expertise, middle managers are called in for their opinion. They are ushered into the top-management circle and exercise some, but not too much, influence. Third, there is a sense of security in being seen as an expert. Senior people seek them out for an opinion. If they weren't there, where would senior managers go to get the answers they need? As one middle manager expressed it:

> I know more about my area than my boss does. He needs me to be there when he has a problem. He knows that I've probably seen it all before.

Once these specialists reach the middle-manager ranks, however, their limited perspective becomes a handicap. They don't have an understanding of the broader context and of the perspective of other functions on many of the issues they must deal with as middle managers. In addition, they are often frustrated by the simple practical problem of not having a network, of not knowing people in other departments when they need to have access to information—a relationship on which to base coordination and teamwork.

Bill Webb at Matco summed up the result of overspecialization as follows:

> When I look at my middle managers, I just don't see any potential general managers out there. We don't move people around any more from department to department and let them gain a wide range of experience and understanding of our business. They don't understand the other person's problems. They view the world through blinders.
>
> It is not their fault. We're the culprits. Their department heads didn't want to let them go because they invested so much in their training and didn't want to have to train people to replace them. We're paying the price for overspecialization now. As I said, the result is that I don't have any people out there right now who have the broad experience required to move up to senior management.

Another perception common in many firms is that the track to the top requires that managers get greater and greater functional expertise. Periodically, articles appear which document that financial people, or lawyers, or marketing experts are now being promoted to the top jobs. Rarely do we hear about how the new CEO of a firm moved through a variety of functions, businesses, and regions, all of which would have enabled him or her to develop the broad base of knowledge needed to handle the myriad of diverse, complex policy and strategy issues that he or she now must face.

This concentration on functional expertise makes integration at the middle-management level more difficult in a variety of ways. It reduces the desire and the need for exposure in other functions. Middle managers concentrate on their own area of expertise—staying on top of that is time consuming enough! Further, they see the world, define problems, and use a vocabulary in terms of their field of specialization. As an example, a marketing person may see poor advertising as the reason for slow sales. A technical person may see a technical limitation of the product. A person from finance may feel the price is too high because the costs are too high—and so on.

This concentration also results in different time frames. R&D feels that years may be the proper time span for measuring results. Marketing may see days or weeks as the appropriate time frame. And, as we mentioned in Chap. 1, senior managers want results before the end of this quarter.

These differences make meaningful communication and common understanding difficult. The issues, words, and priorities are all different. It is hard to appreciate why the other person places so much emphasis on factors we do not see as important from our frame of reference. The phrase "he or she doesn't understand" is an accurate reflection of why middle managers find collaborative networks so difficult to build.

Fragmented Responsibility

Lou Lataif, formerly President of Ford Europe and now Dean of the School of Management at Boston University, describes a recent conversation with the CEO of a major U.S. manufacturer that illustrates the problem of fragmented responsibility. Following an intensive meeting with the senior functional heads of the company, he commented:

> I seem to be the only person around here who is worried about the corporation's bottom line.

The issue of narrow concentration that we have been discussing is not the only barrier to building collaborative networks. The organizational structure itself, which groups people into departments, fragments the sense of responsibility for the goals of the overall organization. The focus of middle managers is often on their department's goals, not the organization's goals. This fragmented responsibility leaves few feeling responsible for the success of the whole corporation. If there is no overall, powerful reason to coordinate, each department will go its own way.

For example, and we will exaggerate here to illustrate our point, the Marketing Department sees marketing as the center of the organization. Middle managers here view heaven in terms of high-quality products, all shapes and sizes, unlimited flexibility and inventory, low prices, special incentives, extended credit, and large advertising budgets. If you don't like blue, we have red. Special orders? No problem! Sure that model is in stock, you can have it tomorrow. Middle managers in Marketing concentrate on the special interests of the customers and are always preparing to respond as the customers continually change their minds.

The middle managers in the Finance Department, on the other hand, focus on finance and control. Their view of heaven is no inventory, cash sales, no financing, and high prices. Better still, let's sell products before we have to make them. Get customers to pay up front, take their cash to buy the raw materials, and produce the product they want. Finance lives in a world of costs and profits, where expenses must be controlled, and fluctuations in interest rates and exchange rates mean the difference between failure and success.

In the Production Department, however, middle managers are concerned with meeting schedules and quality targets. They want virtually unlimited stocks of supplies, qualified workers, the latest technology, predictable demand, and no interruptions for special orders. They want one style, one size, one configuration, so they can turn the production line on and let it run forever. Middle managers in Production live in a world where costs and schedules reign supreme—costs and schedules obtainable by limiting the number of products sold.

Of course, the problem is that the combination of fragmented responsibility and divergent concentration creates a situation where nobody "owns" progress toward the overall goal except those people at the top. Middle managers in Marketing do marketing, in Finance they do finance, and in Production they do production. No one does business. Commitments are to the department, not to the organization. Why integrate across functions? A threat to the business is not seen as a threat to *my* department. Nor is a threat to another department seen as a threat to *my* department and vice versa; so, again, why integrate?

In a crisis situation, such as a large drop in market share or profits, the middle managers in Marketing will mount ad campaigns and extend credit terms. If nothing improves, they will retreat into their own department, feeling that they have done their best in light of their department goals. Middle managers in Finance will follow a similar parochial approach. They will attempt to impose budget constraints and expenditure restrictions that have the effect of inhibiting the actions of other departments.

In this situation, middle managers in Production will push for predictability and limit the number of products and features so much that the company will not be able to respond to changing customer requirements. Each department feels it has done its job as measured against its goals. There is little incentive to work together. Their focus is on different pieces of the puzzle. The company may be crumbling while the various departments smugly point to their accomplishments and blame everyone else for not doing their jobs. The conflict and lack of sharing information across the middle can gradually grind the firm to a halt.

Too Much Analysis, Not Enough Synthesis

In most organizations, the general manager is the person who must make the key decisions. It's not your colleague down the hall or the group you play softball with. Real information, not informal scuttlebutt, goes to the boss. And if you are not the general manager, your job—beyond taking care of your direct area of responsibility—is to prepare analyses for your boss. The boss expects your expert advice and support. He does not expect you to integrate information across departments or to take responsibility for action. That's his job. Middle managers manage their area and answer their bosses' questions with data.

General managers often collude with their middle managers in this disincentive to build collaboration by requiring analyses focused solely on their functional areas. Faced with a problem, middle managers concentrate on providing the information the boss needs within their area. Their job is to provide information, not synthesis.

The result is a downward and inward focus. Networks outside the limited functional area are not necessary. Because middle managers have been asked to do analysis, they have no reason to become part of a network or team to exchange information or to identify different perspectives and points of view. The middle manager's job is to analyze information and, then, to pass the results upward, not across.

It's Natural to Manage Vertically

In the sense that most of us (at all levels) are attuned to our boss and what he or she wants, we focus a large proportion of our time and energy on managing the boss. Our orientation is vertical—upward to our boss or downward to our subordinates—not across. The boss gives us formal information direction, pay increases, and promotions—not our peers in other departments. The boss is the embodiment of the organization to us, not our peers.

Our peers do provide informal social and collegial rewards, but these are for everything except the formally assigned projects and problems. The formal and informal networks do not serve the same purposes. To have middle managers integrate around formal decisions isn't readily done in the up-down organization—that would complicate responding to the person who really counts, the boss. Most people today still work in up-down organizations, not horizontal ones. Our job descriptions always tell to whom we report and who reports to us, not how or which peers we work with. Appraisals are given to us by our boss and signed off by his or her boss. Promotions, new assignments, all come from above, not across. It is little wonder that most of our time and energy goes into managing our boss. As we see it, our future depends on it. Working laterally across the organization, when it might divert our attention from responding to our boss, is a distraction.

Finally, one of the Factors (#7) from our study where a gap was more evident for middle managers than for those above or below them was in career development.

Career Development in the Up-Down Organization

Trapped in the Middle?

For some middle managers, the feeling of being walled in reflects this specialist trap. They feel that their mobility is limited. They lack the broader experience that would open up the career path to a senior-management position. Their options have narrowed. If they decide to make a radical change and leave their area of specialization, they would undoubtedly have to take a cut in pay and accept a lower status in the organization.

In some instances, the pressures of the merge and purge syndrome have completely altered the psychological contract between the middle manager and his or her company. The traditional, paternalistic notion that you would be taken care of if you did a good job is a casualty of the New Competitive Reality. For many who have been merged and then purged, it is a cruel memory. For those middle managers who have survived, prospects are diminished as well.

In their rush for efficiency and in the effort to disband fiefdoms and make staffs leaner, one of today's most popular prescriptions is to reduce the number of managerial layers. For middle managers, this approach represents removing a number of the rungs in the promotional ladder.

The Other Side of the Coin

Amid all the hand-wringing, however, it is appropriate to understand that there can be two sides to this coin for middle managers. One side is the downsizing and disruption brought about by the end of the fiefdoms and the advent of cost cutting. At the same time, the other side of the coin emanating from the New Competitive Reality represents opportunity.

Those middle managers who remain in today's leaner organizations have the opportunity to take on more responsibility, to become more equal partners in meeting the challenges facing American businesses. As we have suggested, they represent the key to the continued recovery of American competitiveness.

Yet, for middle managers to be effective, it is clear that their roles and responsibilities must be redefined. Organizations will have to recognize that their current structure and procedures are inhibiting the effectiveness of middle managers and restricting their ability to shoulder more of the management load. Managers at both the senior and middle levels will need to take steps to alter their firm's structure and procedures in order to clarify and support the new role and responsibilities of middle managers.

It is also clear that middle managers will have to develop new capabilities to meet the new demands of their changed roles and responsibilities. As these elements in their jobs change, they need to learn the broader skills and capabilities the new environment requires. The renewal of middle managers involves learning new skills and developing new capabilities, and it also requires the commitment of senior managers to a recognition of the need to alter the structure and procedures of their firms to support this new role and allow it to develop and grow.

We now turn to the life of middle managers in a new and different world: that of the "balanced" organization.

Endnotes

1. Tracy Kidder, *The Soul of a New Machine*, New York: Avon, 1981, p. 109.
2. Richard Pascale, *Managing on the Edge: How the Smartest Companies Use Conflict to Stay Ahead*, New York: Simon and Schuster, 1990.
3. Rosabeth Moss Kanter has written two excellent books on this subject. The first, which we mentioned in Chap. 2, is *The Change Masters*, New York, Simon and Schuster, 1983. The second is *When Giants Learn to Dance*, New York: Simon and Schuster, 1989.
4. This conflict over turf issues is described in "Donna Dubinsky and Apple Computer, Inc.," a Harvard Business case, #9-486-083 by Mary Gentile and Todd Jick, 1986. John Sculley also cites this conflict between two middle managers in his entertaining autobiography, *Odyssey*.

5
Knocking Down the Walls

In recognition of the growing complexities and increased pace of the New Competitive Reality, the senior managers of many U.S. firms have delegated decisions about operations to middle managers, who are closer to operations and to the customer. The decision to decentralize is based on the sound principles that involvement, participation, empowerment, and ownership motivate people.

However, as we evaluate this effort today, we can see that many attempts to improve organizational effectiveness by giving more responsibility to middle managers are not working. In many firms, vertical channels are still overloaded. Decisions are not being made any faster, and foreign competitors are still able to introduce new products faster than many U.S. firms are.

Balanced Is Better

As we have indicated, the data from our survey suggest that the problem is focused at the middle-manager level. Further, what we found shows that *those firms that have become competitive understand that the move to give more responsibility to middle managers must be accompanied by changes in an organization's structure and procedures.* In turn, these changes support the new roles and responsibilities of middle managers.

The senior managers in these competitive firms have added new dimensions to the structure of their organizations, creating a *balanced organization*. The balanced organization has two added lateral dimensions for middle managers:

1. The first is a horizontal, or lateral, dimension *inside* the organization, flattening the walls of the old "up-down" firm that had separated one department from another.

2. The second is the creation of networks *outside* the organization, spanning traditional boundaries to improve access to new technology and to develop better communication and collaboration with suppliers and customers.

They have added a lateral structure enabling middle managers to develop horizontal networks that cross traditional departmental boundaries. The need to add this lateral dimension was clearly demonstrated in our study that called attention to inadequate lateral information sharing and cooperation at the middle-manager level.

Life is different for middle managers in the balanced organization. We are not suggesting that these balanced organizations have eliminated the vertical dimension. Rather, they have engaged in a realignment of their organization's structure to add the lateral dimension.

The Vertical Dimension: Remaking the Relationship with the Boss

While the vertical dimension of the up-down organization remains, it is different in many ways. The middle manager's relationship with the boss as well as with subordinates is changed.

Beginning in the next chapter, we outline the steps involved in the transition from the traditional, up-down firm to a more competitive, balanced organization. First, however, in this chapter we describe what life is like for middle managers in the balanced organization. Using examples, we indicate how middle managers in these organizations:

1. Function with fewer hierarchical levels and more distributed decision making;

2. Build multiple network links inside and outside the organization; and

3. Assume responsibility for their own, self-directed careers.

One characteristic of the balanced organization is that the middle manager is more on his own. The relationship with the boss undergoes some fundamental changes. Further, what is true for the relationship between a middle manager and his boss is also applicable in many ways to the relationship between the middle manager and subordinates. For both the middle manager and his or her boss, these changed relationships require new roles. As Charles Handy, the much-admired British writer on management, has observed:

> The new manager is a teacher, counsellor and friend as much or more than he or she is commander, inspector, and judge.[1]

This view underscores that we need to make major changes in our way of managing. Our perception of what an effective manager does changes not because managers decide to give up being "commanders, inspectors and judges" in an effort to be popular. Rather, the shift in these relationships reflects the requirements of today's more competitive world.

Moving responsibility for operating decisions down in the organization is a response to the complex requirements of today's marketplace. Consequently, *in the balanced organization a middle manager is much more of a partner with senior management than he used to be. Instead of becoming less important, as was the common view in the merge and purge era, he is now of greater significance to the success of the organization.*

Colgate: From Foxholes to Partnerships

The changing role of middle managers is illustrated by the new organization Reuben Mark has been building since he took over the reins of leadership at Colgate in the mid-1980s. Colgate is an example of a firm that has long had an international orientation, garnering well over half its profits from outside the United States.

In the 1970s, David Foster, then chief executive at Colgate, made a number of acquisitions aimed at increasing the company's size and hence its marketing "muscle" in the competitive struggle with Procter & Gamble. Foster was an autocrat who ran everything from the top. Being a middle manager at Colgate in those days meant that you had to abide by the "foxhole theory of management"—which meant staying in your own foxhole and keeping your head down.

As Colgate's profit progress faltered in the early 1980s, Foster resigned, and Keith Crane took over as chairman. Crane undertook a divestment program, selling off a number of operations that Foster had acquired in the previous decade. Crane's successor, Reuben Mark, has continued the "leaning down" program and has put Colgate back on the path of solid earnings growth. Mark's decentralized approach to decision making is the antithesis of Foster's authoritarian, top-down style. In a recent interview, he said:

> The job [of the chief executive] today is to set a strategic direction, get
> people to agree, give them money and authority, and leave them alone.[2]

Clearly, from the perspective of middle managers at Colgate, foxholes
are out; delegation, autonomy, and trust are in. Middle managers are no
longer expected to simply follow instructions and stay out of the way.
Instead, they are seen as taking on vital responsibilities in their company's
efforts to operate effectively in widely diverse markets around the globe.

Getting Information to Middle Managers

In the balanced firm, senior managers understand that middle managers
need to have access to a great deal more information about the firm's
activities—especially outside their own departments—than was the case in
the up-down organization where their responsibilities were more narrowly defined within the more limited frame of their own function.

In recognition of their new roles, middle managers in balanced companies have access to the following types of information:

1. The strategic plans and market-position objectives of senior management,

2. The action plans of other departments,

3. New product plans from research and development and from marketing,

4. An analysis of trends in market share and the positions of competitors,
   and

5. A report of up-to-date operating and financial results in relation to
   budget.

When decisions are moved down in the balanced organization, new
channels for information sharing are established. At Salesco, for example, senior management decided to extend the process of communicating
its strategy and business plan by including middle managers in management conferences where the *details* were openly shared and discussed.

For some firms, this step of providing middle managers with information previously regarded as confidential by top management represents a
key hurdle on the track to becoming a balanced organization. For instance, at one firm we were told:

> If we give out this information, our competitors may obtain vital facts
> about our plans and objectives.

To this attempt at secrecy, we responded:

> There aren't many secrets among competitors. You can figure out what you would do if you were in their position, and vice versa. So the only people in the dark are those in your own organization, and they are the people you really need to keep informed.

We understand that the process of providing information takes time. Yet, at Salesco, the senior managers found that the added time middle managers spend in this process is more than offset by the increase in effectiveness that results when middle managers are better informed.

Remaking the Relationship with Subordinates

In the process of restructuring, many of the firms we have worked with chose to reduce the numbers of hierarchical levels in their organizations. This process, known as delayering, has had its biggest impact on middle-management levels, where not only are there fewer people but those remaining also have different responsibilities and roles than was the case in their prior lives in the up-down organization.

The Nummi plant in Fremont, California, is an example of an organization where the traditional role of middle managers has been turned on its head. Nummi, an acronym for New United Motor Manufacturing, Inc., is a joint venture between General Motors and Toyota that produces light trucks and Corollas at an old GM plant. This plant, in Fremont, California, was reopened in 1985, after a three-year shutdown, with Toyota managers at the helm.

While the Nummi plant in Fremont has received a great deal of attention, our particular focus here is on the changed role of middle managers in the organizational structure. At Nummi, there are only 6 different levels, from the production workers on the floor to the general manager of the plant, in contrast to 14 levels in a typical General Motors assembly facility.

Middle managers represent only two of the six levels. Not only are there fewer middle managers at these levels, but their responsibilities are very different. Instead of serving as directors, controllers, and checkers, at Nummi middle managers serve as advisers and resources for the workers on the production floor.

To accomplish their assignments, the middle managers at Nummi are expected to spend more than 50 percent of their time out of their offices and on the production floor. The aim is not to tell production workers what to do and then check up on them, but rather to be helpful in resolving problems.

One of the reasons that the role of middle managers has changed in this arrangement is that a great deal more responsibility and authority has been delegated to the work force than is true at the traditional up-down firm. At Nummi, workers on the floor are largely autonomous, controlling everything from the paced work flow to quality control. Computer terminals are located all along the production line, providing data—not for the Management Information Systems Department and senior management—but for the use of the assembly workers on the line.

At Nummi, many of the decisions formerly reserved to middle managers are now the domain of workers on the floor. In addition, under the Nummi system, the decision of a middle manager can be overturned by a vote of four fifths of the employees at the next level below. Authority is no longer the source of a middle-manager's power.

With many of the traditional assignments of middle managers now assumed by workers on the line, the role of middle managers is very different under this approach. For many middle managers accustomed to the traditional pattern of hierarchical authority, the adjustment to a different role has been a difficult one. As Cummins Engine found when they gave a great deal of responsibility and authority to semiautonomous work groups in several new plants, the people who had the greatest difficulty adjusting to their new roles were the plant's middle managers.

In the balanced firm, the role of middle managers is changed. Their assignment no longer involves being a conduit from senior management, bringing instructions and checking up to assure they are followed. Now, instead, the role of middle managers is to remove barriers so that their subordinates can function effectively. Their new job is to provide support that will enable workers on the production floor, or in the field, to do their jobs productively. To do so requires different skills from those traditionally associated with being a middle manager.

As this discussion of the vertical dimension suggests, a middle-manager's relationship with his or her boss and subordinates is changed from the traditional pattern. Just as clearly, in the balanced structure the lateral dimension takes on much greater importance for the middle manager. In turn, the barriers must be removed so that middle managers can function effectively are lateral as well as vertical.

We agree with Tom Peters that one of the major deficiencies in the way American corporations function is that middle managers spend 75 percent of their time operating through vertical channels.[3] He believes that the lateral dimension is more important and that the emphasis should be reversed. Peters argues that organizations should have their middle managers spend 75 percent of their time performing laterally in integrating roles—information sharing, coordinating, and collaborating with middle managers in other functional departments.

Integration in the Middle as Well as at the Top

In many organizations, top managers do not understand the importance of the integrative function of middle managers. In these firms, people at the top are responsible for lateral integration of functions, and middle managers are seen as operating only in a vertical dimension.

In the balanced firm, however, integration takes place at the middle-management level as well as at the top of the organizational pyramid as shown in Fig. 5.1.

Although top management clearly retains the responsibility for the coordination and integration of *strategy*, the process of delegating many decisions related to *operations* to middle managers suggests why integration is needed in the middle as well.

To enable their middle managers to manage their new roles and fulfill their broader responsibilities as integrator, balanced firms have added a number of supporting structural arrangements that we describe in the next section.[4]

The Lateral Dimension: Knocking Down Walls

In the balanced firm, new lateral structures have been added to the long-established vertical ones. In addition to the vertical channel of the boss above and subordinates below, middle managers must develop a lateral network if they are to do their jobs effectively.

Figure 5.1. Management levels and integration.

Balanced firms add a number of structural arrangements that enable their middle managers to establish a network inside *and* outside the organization. These structural elements include:

1. Cross-functional operating teams,

2. Lateral project and new-product teams,

3. Rotation of middle managers across departmental barriers,

4. Cross-functional forums of middle managers, and

5. Human-resource systems that support and value lateral contributions of middle managers.

In describing the development of the lateral dimension, we highlight the nature of structural support for middle managers at Matco, Salesco, and Techco—as well as at a number of other firms.

At Techco, for example, broad assignments and responsibilities were given to cross-functional teams. Using teams in this way enabled Techco to respond more quickly and completely to customer problems.

In an effort to develop an organizational structure that reflected the complexities it faced in engineering and production, Boeing has long assigned the responsibility for specific component systems of an aircraft—such as the wing or tail—to cross-functional teams.

A recent successful innovation at the auto companies is the use of cross-functional new-product teams (PDTs), which have provided middle managers with a broader understanding of problems from a perspective outside their own department. The PDTs collaborate on new products from the earliest stage in the design-engineering process to the actual production of a component or group of parts for a new automobile. These teams include middle managers in a variety of functions, such as design engineering, production engineering, purchasing, finance, marketing, and—frequently—from an outside supplier.

Cross-functional teams have also been utilized by a number of firms that have developed a process known as simultaneous engineering. Middle managers at Hewlett Packard and Ford, for example, have shifted from a sequential process to a simultaneous one that requires continuous information sharing and cooperation in a lateral dimension across departmental boundaries. This shift from a sequential approach to a simultaneous one requires far more information sharing and coordination at the middle-manager level.

This approach is being used successfully at Techco. As a result of delegation and an increased use of cross-discipline teams of middle managers, the time required to introduce products has been reduced significantly. Techco no longer trails its foreign—or domestic—competitors in this vital area.

Although these teams are established with specific functional purposes in mind, a by-product of their use is that they have become an effective way for middle managers to further develop their skills as managers of people. Through participation on one or more teams, they have learned to accept new responsibilities, have gained experience in team-building, and developed a broader understanding of issues from a firmwide perspective.

Building Lateral Networks

We have found that the process of developing a broader perspective of the organization and building a network across departments cannot be left to middle managers themselves to initiate. Rather, senior management must take a proactive role in instituting such communication mechanisms. To be successful, a number of approaches are needed.

To begin with, many companies like Procter & Gamble, GE, and General Foods have *rotation programs* that move a number of middle managers through different functions: finance, marketing, human resources, manufacturing, engineering, and so forth. This process permits them to acquire an understanding of their peers' viewpoints and helps them establish their own communications network. Later, when they need information or someone to collaborate with on resolving a problem, they can contact people they have worked with before.

We have found that rotation plans may meet with resistance from middle managers who are concerned that they may become lost "somewhere in Siberia." To be successful, rotation programs need the involvement of top managers. Consequently, we recommended that Lars Nelson, the head of Techco, establish a rotation plan that would be clearly identified as his program. Accordingly, he is directly involved in selecting participants from among highly rated middle managers. To overcome the concern about becoming forgotten, Nelson holds regularly scheduled meetings with the middle managers in the rotation plan.

In balanced organizations, *lateral moves* are increasingly common. We have seen a number of lateral shifts that have benefited both the organization and the individual. In one instance, designers are rotated into Engineering in order to give them a better appreciation of the product-development process. After several years, they are moved back to positions in Design where they can take advantage of their engineering experience.

Another useful lateral move is geographic. Companies seeking to become more global in their orientation gain significantly by moving Europeans to the United States, U.S. managers to South America, and so on. One issue that these companies must be sensitive to, outside of disrupting family lives, is the reaction of employees in the host country. It is important that they not feel as if they are simply at a way station for up-and-coming managers from overseas.

Further, there is another point of caution that should be considered in programs involving rotation and lateral moves. We have found that it is important for middle managers to stay in an assignment long enough to be accountable for their actions. This usually requires at least a two-year stay. With these caveats in mind, balanced organizations have come to use lateral moves widely and have found that they are healthy for both the managers involved and their firms.

The balanced organization also uses cross-functional teams and project task forces to achieve these same goals. Again, preparation is necessary. At Salesco and Matco, new training programs were added so those involved would gain a thorough grounding in team building, interpersonal skills, and task-force management. At companies ranging from Apple Computer to International Paper and General Motors, this training proved to be so valuable that these programs were soon oversubscribed.

We have found that the teams that function most effectively in the balanced organizations have several important ground rules. One is that the people on these teams need the authority to speak for and commit the departments they represent. In addition, knowledge and information—rather than rank—should be the basis for influence on task forces and cross-functional teams. Our experience at Techco with the teams focused on customer service confirmed that for a team to be effective, its members, regardless of their rank, have to be able to speak for their home units.

Another approach to building networks, a cross-functional forum for middle managers, was established at Matco. This group consists only of middle managers who meet at monthly intervals. The responsibility for the agenda for each meeting rotates among Matco's six departments. Middle managers make presentations and conduct discussions about common concerns and problems. Senior managers attend only when they are asked to comment on a particular issue.

Reaching Outside

In the balanced firm, not only are the barriers between departments coming down, but they are also being removed between groups outside the organization as well. Here again, the advantages of cooperation are winning.

As noted earlier, in 1984, we were involved as consultants in one illustration of this shift—the initiation by General Motors of a New Part- nership with its outside suppliers. The experience of the past suggests that GM took advantage of its muscle to put its suppliers in a subservient position, virtually dictating prices and conditions to the suppliers. GM was not looking for any input from the supplier about materials, specifica- tions, design, and so forth. In 1984, Ray Campbell, a middle manager in charge of Purchasing at the Chevrolet-Pontiac-Canada Division (CPC), began a process of altering this traditional antagonism. Campbell recog- nized that the company could benefit competitively from a less adversa- rial and more cooperative two-way relationship with its suppliers.

Campbell decided to change the dialogue from a "preach at" to a cooperative attempt to develop changes that would ultimately benefit CPC's customers. The major focus of this activity is at the middle- manager level. Middle managers from suppliers are now included on product-development teams so that their input is considered right from the start of the development process.

In addition, Campbell organized a Suppliers Council as a forum for discussing a wide range of issues. The Council developed into a fruit- ful conduit for the company to listen to and get feedback from on how its past actions have hindered the suppliers from producing high- quality, low-cost parts for GM's cars. As a next step, the Council moved ahead to explore ways these barriers can be removed.

Another example of lateral integration across organizational bound- aries is the arrangement between a small, but world-leading, firm in infrared sensing technology and a large manufacturer of aircraft and equipment for space flights. The larger company established an R&D fund for the smaller firm, which agreed to work exclusively with them in this particular technical area. The work began with the two firms jointly developing a 10-year plan for the technology. In turn, this plan became part of the larger company's overall business strategy.

We found that the small firm responded very positively to the openness of the larger firm. The feeling of partnership, especially apparent be- tween the middle managers of the two companies, made all the differ- ence. These firms had collaborated on similar work before, but not with such productive results. The difference was a partnership that lowered the barriers between the two organizations.

Evaluation and Rewards

In balanced organizations, evaluation and reward systems incorporate these new lateral roles. To reinforce the expectation that middle mana- gers are to develop lateral communication channels and collaborate with other departments, their performance appraisals include their work on teams and their achievements in other integrating tasks.

At Salesco, for example, the performance appraisal system has been expanded to include evaluations from people both inside and outside a department. As the first step in this process, the individual meets with his or her supervisor to decide which peers in other departments will be invited to contribute. After obtaining additional information from these people, the supervisor writes up the appraisal.

Managers can also use rewards to reinforce the importance of teamwork and collaboration. We saw this process work effectively at "Massdesign," a highly respected firm of architects in the Boston area. In general, architects are often individual contributors, who do not work well on teams. Massdesign certainly has some of these people, but it has achieved a high level of teamwork as well.

In addition to the examples set by senior managers, the reward system at Massdesign strongly encourages collaboration and reinforces teamwork throughout the organization. A project leader gets a bonus pool to allocate to his team based on the profit realized at completion. (The leader's bonus is determined by the senior-management committee.) The bonus is distributed to each team member on the basis of an evaluation of both individual performance and teamwork. In the language of ice hockey, assists count as much as goals.

The project leader's distribution of the bonus is reviewed by the management committee that can make modifications based upon an individual's contribution to other activities in the firm outside the team. As a result, collaboration within the team and across teams is sought and rewarded. In one instance, one of the senior managers gave up part of his bonus in recognition of an unusual display of teamwork by a junior member. Although most of the people in the firm did not know the source of the added bonus, the message to everyone was clear: Teamwork counts in the eyes of those doing the counting.

Learning to Adapt: The Self-Responsible Career

As middle managers take on the added role of being integrators, their responsibilities require that they move beyond the traditional specialist orientation of their counterparts in up-down firms. The function of integration requires more generalized skills and broader experience—in addition to the particular, specialized skills that formed the center of their expertise in their more limited, narrowly defined responsibilities in the up-down organization.

Although middle managers in traditional organizations are valued and evaluated for their skills as specialists, in the balanced firm they are valued as well for their ability to function as generalists, to possess a broader perspective and range of skills to meet the responsibilities of their roles as lateral integrators.

For some middle managers, this shift represents a threat to a career-long pattern of development; to others it represents a welcome change and challenge to move beyond the specialist role. These new roles—participating in a new product team, managing a task force, developing a different alliance with a supplier, or coordinating a joint venture with a research-and-development partner—require more generalized management skills.

During the period of more benign competitive conditions two decades ago, middle managers formed a psychological contract based on the idea that "If I work hard and do my job, my company will take care of my career with pay increases, promotions, and the like." The pattern was orderly and predictable.

The era of downsizing and the advent of the merge and purge syndrome has resulted in a renegotiation of this traditional type of psychological contract. The initiative has passed to the middle manager to make sure that he or she has acquired the experience and skills to become a valuable asset to the company.

In the vertical dimension, the role has changed, as we have suggested, from controller to coach and mentor. Authority, derived from passing along orders from the top, is no longer the middle manager's source of power. Instead, the middle manager's influence derives from his or her ability to negotiate the system, remove barriers, attract human and financial resources, and achieve collaborative exchanges with other groups inside and outside the organization.

In this lateral dimension, the middle manager's mobility has increased. Because of slower growth, downsizing, and delayering, promotions up the vertical hierarchy—once predictable—are now problematic. Instead, in the balanced organization, lateral moves are now commonplace. They enable managers to expand beyond their specialized area of expertise, to acquire an expanded knowledge of the organization, and to develop additional skills that make them more useful to their firms.

As the competitive forces intensify and the external environment becomes less predictable, it is clear that organizations—and the people in them—must be able to adapt more quickly. Large, top-heavy bureaucracies do not have the adaptability required by the New Competitive Reality. The balanced organization, on the other hand, has been designed in light of these new requirements. Again, those people whose roles are affected the most are middle managers. They have to learn a new managerial approach. Their ability to do so holds the key to the ability of their organization to adapt and compete.

In Part 3, which follows next, we look at the changes in attitudes and behavior needed to establish a balanced organization. We focus on specific steps that both senior and middle managers can take to reorient the jobs of middle managers. In Chap. 7, we return to EMI to see what steps were taken to address the problems identified in the Prologue. In the concluding Epilogue, we come back to EMI two years later to see what impact these changes had on the effectiveness of the firm.

Endnotes

1. Charles Handy, *The Age of Unreason*, Cambridge, MA: Harvard Business School Press, 1990, p. 132.

2. Ronald Henkoff, "Cost Cutting: How to Do it Right," *Fortune,* April 9, 1990. Henkoff suggests that forward-looking managers are taking a new approach to downsizing that involves reducing the workload, not just the number of people. He calls this approach "right-sizing."

3. Thomas J. Peters, *Thriving on Chaos,* New York: Knopf, 1087, p. 370. Peters has a very useful section in this book called "Reconceive the Middle Manager's Role."

4. John Bush and Alan Frohman, "Communication in a Network Organization," *Organization Dynamics*, Fall, 1991. This article describes in further detail communication in the balanced organization.

PART 3
Leading from the Middle

6

Challenging Top Managers to Unleash the Potential

Previous chapters described what can result from unlocking middle-managers' energies and talents. It is apparent to us that most organizations desperately want and need this sort of power. Why don't they unleash it?

There are many reasons: not being clear on what the problem is; not being sure how to bring about organizational change; lack of support for the changes, and so forth. In this chapter, and the two that follow, we talk about the changes that support a middle manager's contribution, the personal changes that senior and middle managers must make, and the strategies followed at EMI to get more leadership from middle managers.

In this chapter we focus on the behavioral and organizational shifts that can support the middle manager in his new role and what senior managers must do differently. These changes start with shifts to a view of the organization with a less rigid structure, a view of the senior-manager's job as working for the middle manager, and an expectation of action from the middle.

Managing from the Middle Out

The traditional view of organizations is the pyramid or triangle. This reflects a top-down philosophy of how things get done. More recently, bottom-up approaches have been popular. However, top-down and bottom-up consider the top and bottom levels. The complementary perspective that can support leadership from middle managers is middle-out.

Actions, ideas, and directions emanating from the middle percolate through levels above and below. Task forces, product-development teams, and committees composed of middle managers are examples of middle-out mechanisms. Middle management is the starting point for actions to be taken by upper and lower levels. An excellent example of this is Ikujiro Nonaka's article that describes the formation of a team of Honda middle managers who developed Honda City. They were told to create something different and that was about all they were told.[1] They had to set their standards and schedule. They were allowed to operate autonomously. They succeeded beyond what had been expected.

This approach organizes around the task at hand. People are brought together based on the skills and experience they can contribute to the work, regardless of seniority, or rank, or part of the organization they are in. It deemphasizes rank in favor of skills and information pertinent to the problem. In fact, leadership may pass from one person to another as the work progresses through different phases. A hierarchy based on seniority or rank is no longer the basis for the organization's operations. It is information and skills relevant to the task that count. In our age of exploding knowledge and technology development, the information is likely to be in the heads of newly hired or retrained workers who concentrate on their areas of expertise. As such, the structure for doing the work of the corporation is more a function of the organization of skills outside of senior management than it is of the traditional hierarchy. One's position in the hierarchy is secondary to one's knowledge and skills.

This approach to structure is not new. It is "organic" rather than "mechanistic," terms that were introduced decades ago by two Englishmen, Burns and Stalker.[2] Mechanistic structures are characterized by a great deal of specialization of work, formalization of responsibilities, and a predominantly top-down flow of information. The organic structure relies less on specialization and formalization. The flow of information is multidirectional, top-down, down-up, and lateral. The term *organic* implies a fluidity—an ability to change, grow, and evolve as circumstances dictate. The structure is not an end but a means to do the work at hand. Procter & Gamble's former chief executive, John Smale, describes the concept as "when you are going to address a problem, get the people who have something to contribute in the way of creativity, if not direct responsibility. Get them together."[3] Recently at Procter & Gamble, teams based on this principle have been credited with inventing a popular drip-proof cap for Liquid Tide, making Ultra Pampers, and turning Pringles around. This approach is not a luxury of success, it is a prerequisite for success in today's New Competitive Reality. It speeds up action and decisions, and it builds greater commitment and excitement as it yields more effective decisions.

Digital Equipment Corporation is a good example of a company that has an organic structure. (Some would argue that they have even gone too far in that direction, that they are too loosely organized.) Leaders of large critical projects can be drawn from just about anywhere in the corporation. Status symbols are kept to a minimum. Organization charts literally do not exist. Reporting relationships are in a constant state of flux. Ken Olson, former President of DEC, credits this organization approach for contributing to a stream of innovations and a reduction in the time to develop new products. Clearly, however, it needs to be organized enough so people understand how to get a job done.

New Questions for Senior Managers

Most senior managers see their jobs as providing direction, ideas, information, and evaluation. To some extent, that is what they should do, but most senior managers ignore another part of their job—to provide an environment that unleashes the middle manager and removes the obstacles in his way. An excellent example of this is what happened in the Technical Development Division (TDD) of Polysar, a worldwide manufacturer of synthetics, rubber, latex, and chemicals based in Sarnia, Ontario, Canada. In one year, the division went from a demoralized, mediocre unit to a productive, high-energy unit.[4]

What happened to cause the turnaround? At the start, performance was poor, market share was declining, budgets and staff were cut. Some key staff left and those who remained had little self-respect and confidence.

Mark Abbott, a British-born-and-educated scientist who had emigrated to Canada, was appointed head of TDD and charged with turning it around. Mark began his tenure by voicing support for the middle managers at TDD. He saw his role as building confidence and cutting back the bureaucracy so that everyone, but especially middle managers, could do their jobs. He spent much time out on the floor restating and asserting his confidence in their ability to do their jobs and to achieve. He began a newsletter with the specific goal of broadcasting successes. This was not to be the typical whitewashed list of dull events, but rather a personal journal of individual and group achievements. Mark wrote the newsletter himself and distributed it to all TDD employees.

Mark had everyone discuss with their supervisors what they saw as their strengths and job-related interests. The purpose was to give employees a chance to structure their jobs or move themselves into jobs they might perform more effectively. Twice a year, Mark and his staff held a daylong session to discuss what they, as top management, could do to help people improve their performance. What could be eliminated? What reports canceled? What meetings deleted? All in an effort to free people so they could focus their efforts on productive work. The results were exciting. The level of communication within the division increased enormously. Rather than fighting each other and protecting turf, the senior staff began working together as a team.

Mark moved responsibility to lower levels and held everyone accountable for making good business decisions that had a payoff in the marketplace. He did not recruit new people, he helped existing people increase their performance. The output of TDD in terms of innovation, new products, and problems solved, went up dramatically. Within a year, TDD went from the division many were trying to get out of, to the division many were trying to get into. Rather than considering themselves "losers," people viewed themselves as "winners" and gained valuable experience that has served them well. Many have risen to top positions. The performance ethic Mark and his management team put in place continued well after the original team moved on.

The difference was not new middle managers, the difference was the way they were managed. The problem was not finding new talent but unleashing the potential already existing in the current staff. We find in many situations, the problem of energizing people is not a creating problem, not a question of bringing in new people, it is an unleashing problem—determining how to cut back constraints so middle managers can perform. Senior management's main questions to middle managers become:

What can I do to help you perform your job more effectively?

What can I do to help you reduce the time you waste?

What can I take care of for you so you can focus on your job?

These questions are simple enough but they are very difficult to ask. Why? Because they overturn the long-established basis of senior managers' power—control. Let us look at this.

Bases of Power Need to Change

Power can have a broad number of sources. Edgar Schein[5] describes the various sources of senior managers' power as:

Reward/punishment: A manager has the capacity to reward or punish through promotions, resource allocation, job assignments, bonuses, and so forth.

Position: A manager has authority because he occupies a position of authority. Inherent in the position is the right to give orders.

Charisma: A manager is followed because he is able to get people to link emotionally with him through common vision, fears, or beliefs.

Expertise: A manager's expertise is the basis for his authority. He knows a lot about the subject; so he is listened to. Position is of secondary importance.

These are the traditional sources of power. The first three imply control, either directly or indirectly. The reward/punishment and position categories refer to hierarchical control. Charisma implies a certain degree of emotional control.

The expertise source of power has less to do with control and more to do with possession of information; as such, it is consistent with the organic structure we described earlier.

The questions posed earlier are inconsistent with a control base of power. They are not based on a manager's ability to reward and punish nor on control of the middle manager because of a higher position. The source of power of the senior manager who asks these questions is his ability to help the middle manager be more productive.

Control

Currently the two dominant sources of management power are the ability to reward/punish and hierarchical position. Control is the result. As noted earlier, this is evident in most of the systems and procedures of the company: MBO, performance appraisal, compensation systems, and job classifications.

Charles Dunn is a senior manager at a major U.S. industrial company. He worked his way up the ladder and is seen as an effective producer. The organizations he manages consistently make their goals. He rarely offers excuses. While not regarded as a team player by most of his peers, he is highly regarded by his superiors because he produces.

Charles's management behavior strongly reflects the assumption of control through the hierarchy. He spends most of his time monitoring results against plans. He meets regularly with his staff to hear how well they are progressing in relation to their plan. The entire meeting follows the format of each manager reporting his or her goals for the week and what has been sold and shipped.

Innovation isn't prized by Charles. He prefers his people to follow procedures. Energy, he feels, should be put into setting and achieving high goals. When performance does not match plan, Charles becomes very concerned and works with that manager to get his or her results on track. He is respected by his managers, who also feel intimidated by him.

To reinforce his control orientation, Charles has adopted the concern for quality being pushed today in many U.S. corporations. He has established quality measures, such as the number of defects per thousand parts, as another set of performance measures that are reported by his managers. If they do not make their targets, he demands corrective action plans and monitors them more closely.

Managers who get ahead, under Charles, are those who achieve their goals. They aren't regarded as creative or as people developers. They are seen as tough, disciplined executives who leave you alone if you make your goals and who are "all over you" if you do not.

Charles's behavior isn't atypical in most corporations, nor is it in any sense wrong. It is what is necessary for an effective organization, but it is not an approach that takes full advantage of the potential of middle managers to provide leadership.

Management of middle managers through senior manager control removes the incentive and initiative for leadership from the middle. It says to the middle manager, "You do what I tell you because I am your boss. You work for me."

In sharp contrast to the control style of management is the enabling style. The enabling style says to middle managers, "You know what needs to be done; I will help you do it." In this light the questions posed earlier are consistent with the style of management.

What can I do to help you perform your job more effectively?

What can I do to help you reduce the time you waste?

What can I take care of for you so you can focus on your job?

Enabling

For leadership from the middle to develop, an orientation different than the one Charles displayed is required. Dick Donnelly is another senior-level manager at the same company. He, too, is regarded as an excellent manager but his style baffles some people. His colleague, Charles, sees him as "soft" and "weak." In turn, Dick sees Charles's style as "overbearing."

Dick does not rely on the hierarchy to get the work done. He does not believe meetings should be consumed by reports of progress against plans. He uses one staff meeting a month for guests to discuss new approaches, practices, or ideas. He takes his managers once a year on visits to other companies to learn what others are doing. He expects his managers to know what the competition is doing and to have action plans to surpass them.

What can I do to help you better achieve and surpass your goals?

Dick is known to regard learning and growth as highly as he values goal achievement. Dick used the company's quality thrust as an opportunity to share with his staff the company's competitive challenge and to ask them to look for and adopt the most effective approaches wherever appropriate. He asked his staff to set quality goals and to tell him what resources they needed from him. He expects the managers to keep track of their own performance and goals and to be responsible for the actions necessary to attain them.

When a manager does not achieve his or her plan, Dick regards it not as a black mark, but as an opportunity to learn and grow. He works with the manager to look at why results fell short and to assess what needs to be changed. If improvement does not occur, Dick tries to move the person to a position that is a better match for his or her abilities.

Dick sees his responsibility as a senior manager to be an "enabler" for his staff. He believes they must generate the ideas, set the goals, lead the teams, and measure the results. He expects them to show initiative, and he manages so they can. His organization consistently produces new ideas and initiatives that become models for the rest of the organization. Do Dick and his managers make mistakes? Sure they do, but the mistakes are regarded as the price for innovation and adaptation to the New Competitive Reality.

Dick's style allows for and, in fact, promotes leadership from the middle. It is in sharp contrast to Charles's. Charles gets conformity to plan and procedures. His organization produces "no surprises." The middle managers do what is expected.

Strengthening the Base of Power

We are not suggesting that Charles Dunn needs to become a Dick Donnelly. He could not, even if it were necessary. What Charles can do to get the best of both a control and an enabling style is to adopt some of the behaviors of the enabling style. Both he and Dick need an effective balance of both behavior styles. Table 6.1 identifies some of the behaviors each could try to emphasize, more of some or less of others, to arrive at a sound balance.

Behavior is difficult to change. Some of what managers do is simply a

Table 6.1. Actions That Strengthen Each Base of Power

Control	Enabling
Expressing approval and disapproval	Expecting and inviting contribution
Clearly stating demands	Building on other's ideas
Setting standards	Encouraging
Rewarding	Praising
Punishing	Showing enthusiasm
Monitoring	Showing confidence

reaction to what is happening around them. However, most of it is based on the values and experiences of a lifetime. The behaviors listed in either column of Table 6.1 will not be easy to adopt if a manager is not accustomed to using them. Behavior is based on ingrained values, beliefs, and habits. Change takes practice and patience. The best way for a manager to begin is to consciously practice using one or two desired behaviors more frequently.

The control behaviors clearly establish expectations and consequences for success and failure. The enabling behaviors tend more to establish a challenge and provide support for stretching.

To motivate using more or less of the behaviors in either column requires starting with an honest self-assessment, asking:

1. What do I do well? What do I want to improve?

2. In which type of situations am I most comfortable and effective? Are they characterized by relying on control or by enabling others?

In addition to a manager's own assessment, he or she should ask others. While peers and colleagues may be reluctant to give candid feedback, they should know that the manager is sincerely interested in their opinions. There are standard questionnaires that provide this kind of feedback, and they can be filled out anonymously. Outside consultants can also collect and feed back this kind of data.

It is important that managers get this type of data so they know where they stand and what type of behavior they should be doing more or less of. One way to keep track is to tally the frequency of whichever behaviors they are trying to do more often. For example, if a manager wants to do more encouraging and praising, at the end of every day, or when it is convenient, that manager should count up how often he or she encouraged or praised someone. Over the course of several weeks it can be determined if the daily average increases.

If senior managers can achieve an appropriate balance between enabling and controlling, they will release tremendous energy from the middle ranks. But, this is not all that must change. Managers hold some beliefs that are inconsistent with leadership from the middle. These, too, need to be examined and revised. The beliefs and strategies that must replace them are discussed next.

Supporting Beliefs That Must Change

In this section we discuss four prevailing beliefs that must end and the new beliefs that must replace them if leadership from the middle is to come into being. These prevailing beliefs reflect traditional management values that are inappropriate for the New Competitive Reality.

The four prevailing beliefs that must change are:

- A problem can be solved by focusing solely on results.
- Competition is healthy and gets the most out of people.
- The solution to most problems is getting (or cutting) resources.
- Things cannot change until top management changes the way it manages.

Unleashing leadership from the middle is hindered by these beliefs. Leadership from the middle requires a different set of supporting beliefs, namely:

- Focus on changing the process rather than the end results.
- Focus on collaboration rather than competition as the means to better performance.
- Focus on the new ways to use the resources rather than on getting (or cutting) resources.
- Focus on leadership from the middle rather than waiting for top management to change before other changes can occur.

To develop these beliefs, managers must initiate new strategies for viewing their corporations and their changing roles in the New Competitive Reality.

Look at How Things Really Get Done

In our society we believe that the best way to approach a problem is to tackle it directly. If the product costs too much to manufacture, look at ways to cut costs; if we are paying too much in salaries, cut the headcount or salaries; if we are too slow with new products, cut down the cycle time. Yes, those are needed, but this approach often is more of a one-shot, quick fix to correct the symptoms rather than a long-term solution. To put in place a more meaningful solution requires changing the process underlying the problem. The manager must attack the problem from a new perspective. For example:

- If the product costs too much, what can be changed in the development process that will result in lower cost: earlier involvement of manufacturing, use of fewer prototypes, better market definition from marketing.

- If the budget for salaries is too high, what can be changed in the hiring, training, and managing process: greater use of teamwork, raising performance standards, better definition of skill level versus work required, and so forth.

- If the product-development cycle is too long, what can be done to redesign the process to shorten it: clearer product specification, greater use of teamwork, fewer hierarchy-laden checkpoints, and so forth.

Names for this type of analysis are root cause, fishbone, and causal analysis. All of these require examination of the process that produces the results. It means looking for the root cause of the problem. Corporate leaders in the United States are more comfortable focusing on managing the numbers, cutting budgets, headcounts, and the like. In the long run this is counterproductive. If leadership from the middle is to take hold, this approach needs to change. Focusing on the numbers allows little latitude for innovation and initiative. It leads to cutting and slashing—not innovation, initiative, and risk taking. If leadership from the middle is to work, it is in changing *how* the work gets done—the hiring process, the product-design process, the product-planning process, the billing process, the purchasing process, and so on.

For years, corporate executives have tried to significantly cut costs. Headcount reductions, budget trimming, and program slashing never seemed to really get to the heart of the problem. Now some are embarking on a new set of initiatives. These activities focus on how the product is designed and engineered, how suppliers are involved, how the production schedules are set, and so on. The question is what could the middle managers do better, not what costs would be cut. While it is too early to judge the success of this new approach, the early results we have seen suggest it is very promising.

Look at the Process of Managing

Once the need to look at the process is understood, what do you do?

To begin with, clearly define what the problem really is and what is causing it. Symptoms (the product costs too much to make) should be separated from causes (product specifications are being changed too often). Push to find the real causes of the problem.

This approach also applies to looking at the administrative and other processes that affect leadership from the middle. Appropriate involvement from the middle ranks can make a significant difference. Some of the processes that can be examined in order to boost leadership from the middle are:

Planning: Who is involved? What latitude do they have? Who do they work with?

Budgeting: Who determines budgets? How do final budgets get set? Once budgets are approved what flexibility is there?

Hiring: Who makes hiring decisions? On what basis are they justified?

Product development: What is the formal process? How many approvals and checkpoints are there? How many approvals are required? Are they all needed?

Training and development: How much emphasis is there on staff development? What is offered to middle managers?

Essentially, looking at three factors—who has the responsibility to make the decisions, who must approve them, and who provides the information for the decisions—will tell any organization most of what it needs to know about its management process. A useful technique for analyzing this is called Responsibility Charting.[6]

If the responsibility for most decisions rests with senior managers, the opportunity for leadership from the middle is reduced. If middle managers have the responsibility for decisions but must pass through multiple layers for approval, again the opportunity for middle management leadership is reduced. Finally, if the middle manager responsible for making a decision cannot or does not get the information he needs to make a well-informed decision, he cannot exercise his judgment in a sound fashion. To boost leadership from the middle, decision making needs to be the responsibility of the middle manager. Whenever appropriate, approvals should be limited only to those who must be involved, and information should flow to the decision maker from anywhere in the organization. The new information technology can make this possible. It can help transform the nature of work and unleash middle managers. The technology can integrate information across units, broadening the focus for all managers and allowing middle managers to exercise initiative not imagined earlier.[7]

Try Collaboration, Not Competition

Middle managers usually do not have all the information, resources, or responsibility to execute any but the most narrow of plans. If middle managers are to provide leadership, it will require support from other middle managers. This will come from a view that if one wins, all win; if one loses, all lose.

Now the prevailing attitude is more one of, "If I win, you lose; if you win, I lose." This breeds adversarial relationships and ensures that decisions get pushed up to the top. Leadership from the middle cannot work in this environment.

In one company, two product managers were responsible for products in neighboring market segments. Each eyed portions of the other's market as a way to gain higher sales volumes. Of course, it meant one would win at the expense of the other. This destructive, noncollaborative attitude was fostered by the planning, budgeting, measurement, and reward process. Plans were done strictly on a product-segment basis. There was no cross-talk from one segment to another to look for areas of synergy or interdependence. Budgeting was based on each manager promising so much against only his own goals—again no credit was given for collaboration or assists. The measurement and reward process looked only at the achievement of the narrow product-segment goals. Further, the goals were stated solely in terms of sales volume. Contributing to company profit and reducing variable costs were not measured. To shift the emphasis from competition to collaboration required changing much of the management process.

In the previous chapter we discussed the importance of collaboration. We want to reinforce this point: Cooperation is not a luxury. It is a necessity. Without it neither the information nor the support to take the initiative exists.

Get More Done with Existing Resources

Another excuse we have heard for not exercising leadership from the middle is insufficient resources. In one company, the project managers all complained that they had too few engineers to meet their schedules. They could not get the drawings out on time. Certainly there was no slack for innovation or loaning people to other projects. The prevailing attitude was that there was no problem that could not be solved with more resources. As we followed this company over three years we watched this attitude shift. The number of programs increased, the actual number of engineers decreased, and the products produced were substantially better. Why? The focus changed from asking for more resources. The project leaders went back to examine the processes they were using for product design, product planning, use of outside vendors, and collaboration across products. No magic—just a different focus underpinned by careful redesign of processes to promote more effective use of the resources of the company. Senior management stopped believing that the answer to getting programs done was finding more money for more engineers.

Don't Focus Just on Getting or Cutting Resources

The attitude that any problem can be solved by adding more people is fostered by the same mistaken thinking behind the merge, purge, and leverage attitude. In both cases the problem is defined as a resource problem. In the first case, too few; in the second case, too many.

No doubt there are legitimate occasions when adding or reducing resources is necessary. But most senior managers (and often middle managers) jump too quickly to this as the solution to the problem. We ask that managers pause before dealing with each problem as a "budget issue" and ask themselves, "If I *had* to make do with these resources, what would I do?" Another question all managers need to ask is, "Is this step, project, or operation really necessary?"

The quick fix is to focus on resources. As noted earlier, this is due to the fixation with control and the desire for visible action. Whether in corporations or public programs, the problem is all too quickly labeled a budget problem. The corresponding course of action, therefore, becomes adjusting the budget. This, in many cases, is fussing with symptoms, not causes. Nor does it foster initiative or leadership. Providing better service to customers, achieving better product or service performance, and bringing out new products faster can lead to middle-manager leadership and initiative.

Quit Waiting for Top Managers to Change

In many companies we hear, "Top management is the major barrier to change. If they would change, then we can change." No doubt this is true. If top management changes, it will be easier for lower levels to change. But there is much that middle managers can do to take the initiative. If they wait for top management to change, they themselves are engaging in behavior that is exactly the opposite of what is required. Further, changes are most effective if they occur in lots of parallel steps that mutually reinforce each other. Change can start anywhere in an organization and spread, as results become evident to others.

We agree that what the top person pays attention to helps set the pattern for what the lower levels will focus on. We do not take lightly the signals top management sends nor the behavior top management supports. It is a powerful lever in shaping the behavior of the rest of the organization. But we have heard too often "they must change first" as an excuse not to do what can and should be done by the middle managers to exercise leadership. The two product managers described earlier, who competed with each other, did not need the company president to tell them they were hurting the company. They could have worked together to optimize their approach to the market. Two product-development team managers fighting each other for the limited pool of designers do not need someone to tell them that no one will win. They have the latitude to examine their work plans to see how the designers can be effectively utilized on both projects. Yes, it would help if top management would change, but it is not a sufficient reason for middle managers not to change. The middle manager must accept responsibility. This is the subject of the next chapter.

Learn to Be Patient

It takes between two and five years for the changes we have described in this chapter to be fully embraced by both senior and middle managers. Everyone needs to be patient to stay the course and see that the small steps forward are taken. Most companies have tried other approaches to improve their results: cutting costs and reducing headcount, but they have not worked. These approaches attack the symptoms, at the expense of solving the problem. The course of action presented here—building leadership from middle managers—perhaps is not any easier and is certainly not a quick fix. But it is a course that builds the kind of organization most senior and middle managers really want, as well as one that deals with the causes of the problems.

Specific Ideas for Unleashing the Potential

1. Walk into the offices of middle managers. Ask them what they think of the organization's goals and strategy. What is their understanding of them; how do they assess progress?

2. Look at how project teams get put together and how work gets done. Can more cross-functional teams be used?

3. Look at how rewards are given out. Do they just recognize performance of the individual (vs. the team or unit) and for performance specific to one functional area? Can this be changed?

4. Identify people who have assisted others above and beyond the call of duty. Publicly acknowledge and reward their action.

5. Ask your people the three questions:
   What can I do to help you perform your job more effectively?
   What can I do to help you reduce the time you waste?
   What can I take care of for you, so you can focus on your job?

6. Get feedback about your style of management from colleagues you trust and respect. Do they see you using more of a control style or an enabling style? Does this vary from one type of situation to another? Start monitoring your use of actions to strengthen the style you want to use more frequently. You might use a form like the one in Fig. 6.1 to get feedback from others.

7. Encourage people to describe what *causes* the problem before they give you solutions. Introduce root-cause analysis to your organization.

8. Set goals that get your staff to focus on the process and skills for doing the work, as distinct from end results.

9. Make sure all plans recognize interactions and impacts with other units and that the other units have been involved in the planning of the activity.

Person to be rated _____

Person doing the rating _____

Directions: Please answer each question candidly. You are being asked for your perception of the behavior of the person to be assessed as you see him or her.

For each behavior, check one of the categories.

	Too Little	*Too Much*	*About Right*
Expresses approval			
Expresses disapproval			
Clearly states demands			
Sets high standards			
Rewards others			
Punishes others			
Monitors others			
Invites contributions			
Builds on others' ideas			
Encourages			
Praises			
Shows enthusiasm			
Shows confidence in others			
Comments			

Figure 6.1. Behavior rating form.

Endnotes

1. For a good description of the work behind the design of Honda City, see Ikujiro Nonaka, "Toward Middle-Up-Down Management: Accelerating Information Creation," *Sloan Management Review*, Spring, 1988, p. 9.

2. A number of researchers have used the terms "organic" and "mechanistic" since then, but T. Burns and G. Stalker, *The Management of Innovation* (London: Tavistock Publications, 1961), are geneally credited with their initial definition.

3. *The Wall Street Journal, Fortune*, and other business publications have carried numerous articles over the last five years praising the shifting of power downward. For example: "CEO's See Clout Shifting," *Fortune*, November 6, 1989, p. 66.

4. This example comes from *Directing Strategy The Keys to High Performance* by Lloyd Baird and Alan Frohman (Englewood Cliffs, NJ: 1992). We have applied a number of the ideas from this book here and in the following chapters.

5. Going back to the 1950s, many authors have described the bases of power. Two of the more contemporary authors are John Kotter and Edgar Schein. Both have helped to clarify and expand the thinking on the use of power. See E. Schein, "Reassessing the 'Divine Rights' of Managers," *Sloan Management Review*, Winter, 1989, and J. Kotter "Power, Dependence, and Effective Management," *Harvard Business Review*, July-August, 1977.

6. Responsibility Charting is described in "Establishing Leadership: How to Analyze and Deal with the Basic Issues," *Management Review*, New York: AMACOM, April, 1980.

7. Shoshana Zuboff, author of *In the Age of Smart Machines*, New York: Basic Books, 1988, does an excellent job of describing the impact of new information technology.

7

Forget About Peter
and His Principle

In this chapter we expand the discussion of current management beliefs and attitudes, especially at the senior-manager level, that must change to support leadership from the middle: the need to reinforce action from the middle, to promote risk taking, and to make developing people a responsibility as important as getting the task done. Next, we revisit EMI to learn what they did to become more competitive by fostering leadership from the middle.

Senior-Management Role:
A Change in Perspective

Reinforcing Action from the Middle

To encourage initiative and innovation from middle managers, senior managers must let it be known that they expect *action*.

Each middle manager must feel a sense of urgency to move the organization ahead. Neither crisis nor opportunity alone will move middle managers to action—they only create the *conditions* for action. People will act based on their perceptions of the situation. Senior managers, not the situation, must reaffirm the sense of action and urgency for the middle managers.

Senior managers can help middle managers identify those factors that can make the most impact if changed. Nobody can do it all; middle managers must know what will make a big difference and what can be changed.

To identify what can make this difference, the problem needs to be clearly identified and its causes understood. If a product isn't selling, is it due to poor advertising? Too high a price? Inappropriate features? Look at what the major causes are and focus on them. Middle managers will not be able to do it all.

Senior managers need to let middle managers know they are counting on them and that they are part of a special group. Middle managers need to know their contributions are essential to making the company successful in the competitive race, not vice versa. It will take some extra effort, and that extra effort is expected and needed. Their success and the company's success depend on their contributions.

In all businesses today, the New Competitive Reality is inescapable. Competition has increased dramatically over the years. Deregulation has intensified competition in financial services, transportation, and communication. Foreign competition has intensified in an endless list of industries. Making sure employees are aware of their competitors, who they are, what they are doing, and how they are doing it is vital for building a sense of action and urgency. Middle managers need to participate in competitive analyses of the functions that are pertinent to their work. If they are engineers, they should know how the competition develops new products; if they are in the Marketing, they should know how the competition sizes up the market. Everyone should be responsible for understanding the competition and then deciding what actions they should take in order to get ahead.

A useful technique is to draw up Spider Charts, named for the spiderweb effect of a completed chart. (See Fig. 7.1.) Along the radii are measures of performance with the target for that measure being the circumference of the circle. The competition and the company are rated on each product, process, or service-performance measure. For example, the five radii for a video recorder might be cost, ease of use, appearance, range, and frequency of repair. On each dimension, the company would rate, as quantitatively as possible, its own product and the best of the competition. (The best of the competition may be supplied by different companies from one radii to another.)

The key, then, is to develop initiatives to close every gap and/or to achieve the target along every radius.

Senior managers can reinforce this by not accepting any analysis without an action recommendation, and by having every team, task force, and committee know their charter is to act. Nothing reinforces initiative like lots of encouragement all along the way. All of us need reassurance that

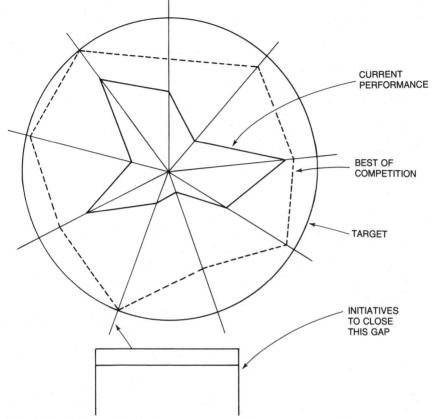

CURRENT
PERFORMANCE

BEST OF
COMPETITION

TARGET

INITIATIVES
TO CLOSE
THIS GAP

Figure 7.1. Program spider chart.

we are on the right track and making progress. Senior managers should not wait for major milestones or completions. It is the little victories that fuel the ultimate victory. The personal touch of a letter, phone call, or visit will be remembered for a long time.

Building up support for taking the initiative can take a long time, but it can be destroyed quickly. We have seen the insertion of a staff group, which analyzes all recommendations for the boss, destroy the support for taking initiative. People had to react to this staff group and prepare for them. This led to more careful control of information, less sharing, and more defensive behavior. It put the emphasis back on analysis rather than on an open discussion of issues and taking action. It resulted in management by fear and intimidation. ITT in the 1960s under Harold Geneen is a well-documented example of this controlling approach to management.

Fortunately, the trend in many U.S. corporations now appears to be in the opposite direction as companies like GE, IBM, and GM move to reduce the size of corporate staffs.

To foster action, it must be recognized that top managers do not solve problems or create information; they provide direction, remove barriers, and unleash energy. The information and energy are diffused throughout the organization; problems get solved and ideas are turned to action by building on the knowledge and capability of people in the organization. For this to occur middle managers must seize the initiative. The success of the organization is directly dependent on the effectiveness of middle-management's initiative.[1]

Promoting Risk Taking

It was the initiative of Art Fry, middle manager at 3M, that led to development of Post-It™ Notes.[2] It was a well-managed risk. The middle manager built up the team and investment in the product slowly. He experimented with its marketing, sending samples to a variety of potential customers. When he finally struck paydirt, getting many orders from secretaries of Fortune 500 CEOs, he knew he had a viable product.[3]

Sometimes middle managers don't seize the initiative because they fear the consequences of failure. They view senior managers as not tolerating mistakes that inevitably accompany trying something new. As one middle manager stated:

> Senior management says they want us to innovate and take risks. They call it "taking measured risks." That means it is okay to take a risk . . . as long as you don't fail.

The reward system in most organizations reinforces a very conservative approach to risk. If a manager backs a proposal that ultimately fails, he may never recover. If he does not support the proposal, and it goes ahead anyhow and fails, he can say he warned them. If he does not support it, and it succeeds, he can say he helped to bring about its success. So, clearly, a calculating manager has much more to lose by supporting a proposal than by rejecting it—hence a tendency to say "no" to new ideas.

Senior managers must actively counter this conservative dynamic. They must serve as models for initiative and risk taking. For example, Frederick Smith set a tone of action and initiative taking at Federal Express when he founded the company in the early 1970s. Smith risked millions of dollars starting up an overnight air-delivery service. He has built the company to annual revenues of over $4 billion, based on his initial risk-taking, which has continued as the company has grown. Not all his ventures have succeeded. ZAPMAIL AM failed miserably in 1984, and the firm lost a lot of money. But this example served as a testimonial to his employees that trying to innovate will sometimes result in failure, and that that is a risk worth taking.

At Hewlett Packard they have an award for "Meritorious Defiance," which is awarded for contempt and defiance above and beyond the call of duty. At Hewlett Packard, courage counts more than obedience. Creating a climate for risk taking requires this attitude. At 3M, managers are expected to take risks with the recognition that many of them will not pay off. People know that when this happens they will not be punished; calculated risk taking is an integral part of the culture. This led to innovations such as the Post-It™ Notes.

Discarding the Peter Principle

To believe in promoting risk taking, we are going to have to give up on the Peter Principle, which is that people rise to the level of their incompetence. It assumes people hit a limit and stop striving. We do not believe this is the case. Managers impose limits by their actions and systems. A failure is viewed under the Peter Principle as evidence of a limit or incompetence. If senior managers are to promote risk taking, failure needs to be viewed as an opportunity for learning and growth.

Rather than managers' assuming people rise to the level of their incompetence and constantly searching for new people who have the skills and motivation needed to replace people who have hit their limit, they should assume people can change, improve, and learn. Then the managers would concentrate on removing restraints and creating conditions that allow middle managers to perform to their existing potential and develop increased potential. Senior managers should not focus on looking for extraordinary managers, but rather on creating conditions for ordinary managers to do extraordinary things.

The senior executives reading this may be nodding, "Okay, I'll tell them it is part of their job to take the initiative and make decisions." Is that enough? One senior executive we know set out to tell every manager to "take the initiative, be champions, make decisions." But his actions did not support his words.

If a middle manager came to him for a decision, he made it. He reviewed all major program decisions and frequently reversed them. When conflicts arose below him, he stepped in to resolve them himself. He let little pass without his thorough review. His managers soon learned he expected to be the decision maker on all important program matters. This behavior is incompatible with expecting leadership from the middle.[4]

Changing at EMI

In the Prologue we introduced the reader to EMI, a company facing a stark future if it did not change. Let us see how they tackled their problems.

The Task Force and Its Objectives

We started by organizing a task force of primarily middle managers across all functional units to begin to get our hands on the problems. Representatives from Manufacturing, Personnel, Purchasing, Finance, Education and Training, Legal, Quality and Reliability were on the task force. We continued to serve as consultants, but now to the task force. The task force was chaired by the vice president of personnel, a capable group leader. The task force reported to David Frank, the president, who in his memo inviting the task force members to participate, indicated that they would be working for him on this task force and that he would be the one to whom they would deliver their report. He indicated that he would be the one responsible for accepting their recommendations. He showed his support by attending the first several meetings, and being available to them throughout their work to respond to questions or to help with communications.

The task force identified three key objectives for their work. Objective 1 was to see that the human resources to achieve EMI's business plan were in place and that performance necessary to achieve the business plan was achieved. Objective 2 was to hold managers accountable for seeing that lateral communication and effective horizontal relationships consistent with high performance occurred. Objective 3 was to develop the policies and procedures to promote the development of high performing management talent for the future. The primary focus was on creating a more horizontal organization. It was felt that doing this would facilitate leadership from the middle managers.

The task force had four principles in developing its recommendations. They were:

1. The recommendations should be consistent with EMI's five-year business plan.

2. The recommendations should focus time and energy in the areas that provided maximum payoff.

3. Where possible, existing programs, systems, and procedures should be used.

4. The recommendations should support ongoing initiatives such as the salary program as well as training programs where possible.

The Challenges

The task force identified three challenges that the organization faced in order to make any progress. The organization was going to have to manage multiple thrusts at once.

The organization was going to be disrupted by adopting new practices and procedures, transitioning from a top-down organization to a more horizontal organization, as well as bringing in and training people in new skills and new practices. At the same time, productivity and quality were going to have to dramatically improve in order for the company to remain competitive. The business plan called for dramatic improvements in performance, while at the same time there were going to have to be dramatic changes in the way the organization operated. Achieving both simultaneously was the first challenge.

The second challenge was that at the same time the pressure on managers for performance was increasing, the managers were going to have to try new and different ways of managing. As pressures for improved productivity increased, managers were going to have to allow subordinates more time for lateral communication, broadening of skills, teamwork, and so on.

The third challenge was that EMI, which had been successful based on a strong functional organization for several decades, would have to establish mechanisms for more effective and broader horizontal communication. These horizontal mechanisms would have to coexist with the vertical ones.

In identifying these three challenges, the task force acknowledged the culture of the current organization as well as the need for change. There were very powerful forces holding current and, in some cases, dysfunctional policies, procedures, and behaviors in place. The task force realized that it had a difficult job in front of it. In addition to identifying the changes that were appropriate, it needed to see that the changes were implemented so they would take hold and stick in spite of conflicting pressures. The task force worked for three months, oscillating between frustration over the current situation and its difficulty in coming up with recommendations that satisfied it and euphoria when it identified lever-age points and actions. Over the course of these several months it met three times with David Frank who responded with encouragement, sup-port, and reminders of how important the group's work was.

This was not a full-time job for any of the task-force members. They spent an average of one or 1½ days a week on work for the task force, while at the same time trying to keep up with their jobs. All the task-force members were selected by David and the vice presidents (the Executive Committee) because of their ability to contribute. They were recognized as being very good performers who could both understand the problems and bring forward bright new ideas to solve them. Fortunately, because of David Frank's strong and very visible support of the task force, there was minimal interference from the rest of the organization with the work of the task force and the time required by its members to carry out their task-force duties. (This had been a problem for previous task forces.) However, more often than not, the task-force meetings started about six o'clock over dinner and went into the night so that they would not interfere any more than they had to with the normal workday.

After three months of work, the task force was ready to report back to the Executive Committee. The task force came up with two categories of actions. First, organizational actions that revolved around the business plan—actions that needed to be taken for the organization as a whole. The second category of actions was for the top managers of the Executive Committee. We'll start by describing the organizational recommenda-tions of the task force and then move to the recommendations for how senior managers' behavior needed to change to support moving from a vertical to a more balanced type of organization.

Actions to Modify the Organization

The first activity of the task force was to look at the business plan in order to determine, based on the objectives and goals for the next five years, where actions would have the maximum payoff. The task force decided that changes needed to be made across the entire organization. In fact, most of the recommendations did encompass the entire organization. But the task force wanted to make sure that effort and energy was focused especially on the key areas where more effective horizontal communica-tion was necessary in order to ensure success of the business plan.

The task force took a critical-factor approach, identifying the factors most critical to the success of the company over the next five years. Three areas jumped out from the business plan.

1. Introduction of new manufacturing technology,

2. Horizontal communication between Engineering and Manufacturing and between Engineering and Marketing, and

3. Building the capability of middle managers.

The first was the introduction of new technology on the factory floor, not necessarily sophisticated robotics or automation, though in some cases this was to be done, but more important, the updating and upgrading of machinery, work techniques, management of inventory, and work flows within the plant. This was key to achieving the productivity increase and faster new-product development time that the company required. The specifics of these recommendations will not be discussed here for obvious reasons. They have to do with the levels of automation appropriate for different operations, the number and types of robots to be used, and the plans for implementation.

Improving horizontal communication was the second critical success factor. The first link was between Engineering and Manufacturing. Improvement was necessitated by the need to introduce new technology into the plant. To be successful, the process engineers and production people needed to work together closely from the outset. Not doing this in the past resulted in new equipment's not being fully effective and, in some cases, in its being scrapped.

The second linkage to be improved was between Marketing and Engineering. The business plan required more careful specification of products, and a wider variety of products in order to sell effectively to market niches. The production run for each niche was much smaller than the usual production runs. As a result, the Engineering-Marketing interface was critical. Marketing was going to have to thoroughly understand what the customers wanted, which would then be translated by the engineers into detailed drawings and blueprints for the development of the product. This did not necessarily require the development of new technology. It did require clear communication and lots of cooperation between Marketing and Engineering. In the past the Marketing-Engineering interface had been characterized more by conflict and contention than by cooperation. Engineering felt that Marketing often asked for things that Engineering said were (a) impossible, or (b) not needed. Marketing's response to what Engineering produced was usually that Engineering overengineered products and came up with neat, gee-whiz gadgets—not really innovations that would make a difference in the marketplace. With the business plan calling for a wider variety of products more closely tailored to the marketplace, tolerance for the past, narrow-minded behavior on the part of either function was over.

Better horizontal communication was important in other areas also—there needed to be good communication with the customers; the training department needed to understand and work closely with all other functional departments in order to provide the development opportunities necessary for successful implementation of the business plan, and so on. But the task force did not want to use an across-the-board, do-it-now approach. This approach was characteristic of programs that the company had undertaken in the past. The task force wanted to focus its energy only on the key strategic areas and to be sure energy was devoted to these areas for the long run. Limiting the number of areas helped to ensure a successful start to reorienting the organization as well as a consistent focus throughout the company.

To improve linkages between Engineering and Manufacturing and between Engineering and Marketing, a team was formed for each. The teams consisted of middle-management representatives from both functions. The charter of each team was to identify blocks that prevented effective horizontal linkages, to develop the action plans to remove those blocks, and to implement those action plans. Each team consisted of seven people.

Recommendations of the Engineering-Manufacturing Team

The Engineering-Manufacturing team came up with three major recommendations for improving horizontal linkages between the engineers and the plant people. Implementation was to occur in three phases, starting with a geographical change. The first recommendation was to move the engineers, where feasible and economically justifiable, to the factory floor, so that they could work more closely with the production engineers and plant people involved in manufacturing the products. This mutual location was seen as important in improving communication between the two groups. The relocation was accomplished by building offices in the production environment for the engineers and providing them with adequate soundproofing and lighting. The engineers still reported to their functional engineering bosses.

The second phase of the plan was to organize the engineers and the plant people by product teams or by plant operation if product teams didn't make any sense. That is, the engineers and plant people responsible for designing, developing and manufacturing the small electric motors were all organized into the small electric-motor team. The engineers and plant people on that team met together weekly and worked together on a day-to-day basis to discuss design, development, production, quality, and delivery of their product. Other organizations have come to call this "simultaneous engineering." This worked very well as the engineers and plant people got to know and understand each other's needs and requirements much better. The time to develop new products and product changes dropped dramatically. Prior to this organization by teams, it took 9 to 12 months to implement most of the product changes in small electric motors. After the product teams were formed, the time was cut to 2 to 4 months, a significant reduction. The main reason for the dramatic improvement was that middle managers were now talking to each other across departmental lines.

The third and final recommendation was carried out one year later. It was to bring the engineers and manufacturing people under one boss. This, in effect, changed what was a functional organization now to a product organization with fewer hierarchical barriers to the flow of work. The heads of the merged Engineering-Manufacturing organization teams were for the most part drawn from the engineering organization. This was done because the engineering organization had more middle managers with the relevant skills and breadth of perspective to manage these teams. This revealed a deficiency in manufacturing middle management that had gone unrecognized until that point.

Up until the organization of the product teams, the absence of the broader perspective on the part of the plant middle managers was not recognized as a problem. With the recommendations to form product teams and then the changes in the organization structure, it became clear that the plant middle managers had been too narrowly focused on the day-to-day production operations to enable them to communicate and work effectively outside their specialties. The uncovering of this problem was seen as an important step forward in the development of the plant middle managers. It was evident that more actions were necessary to accelerate the development and horizontal integration of the middle managers in Manufacturing. These actions included rotation, formal management-development programs, and mentoring assignments for senior-level manufacturing managers.

Recommendations of the Engineering-Marketing Team

The first recommendation of the Engineering-Marketing team was to have selected engineers assigned to Marketing. This was done on a rotating basis where engineers were assigned to work within the marketing organization for a one- to two-year period. The objectives of this assignment were twofold. The first was to let the engineers be the liaisons to their functional unit in order to translate the market needs and requirements for more effective detailing and specification of the product. The second purpose of this assignment to Marketing was for the engineers to help the marketing people ask the kinds of questions that would provide data more useful to the engineers in product design. By rotating the engineers through the marketing organization the problem of not having a career path for engineers within Marketing was avoided. Twelve engineers were assigned to Marketing in the next three months. The engineers assigned were high-potential people jointly selected by the top management of the Engineering and Marketing organizations. These assignments soon resulted in much better horizontal communication as lateral networks between Engineering and Marketing were established.

The second recommendation was to organize Engineering and Marketing by product teams. Engineering had typically been organized by the part of the motor that it worked on. In other words, one group of engineers worked on the electronic controls, another group of engineers worked on the casting, and so on. The recommendation was that the engineers and marketing people be assigned to work by product. This paralleled the recommendation made by the Engineering-Manufacturing team. Most of the same product teams identified in the Engineering-Manufacturing recommendations were identified by the Engineering-Marketing team. Now midlevel manager teams were formed linking all three departments. (The engineers that were assigned to work with the plant people on teams were different engineers than those assigned to work with Marketing. The reason was that product development engineers were more focused on Marketing, whereas production and process-development engineers focused on the Manufacturing organization. These were, in fact, two separate groups within Engineering.)

A year after these recommendations had been implemented, one of the most significant changes was the increased collaboration between Engineering and Marketing. The level of ongoing communication and dialogue was tremendous. The squabbles that constantly existed between the two regarding the effectiveness of product changes and product specifications had all but disappeared. In fact, the vice president of Marketing found that one of the engineers who had been rotated into his organization, Chris Brennan, was one of the most effective marketing people. Chris lit up with the opportunity to go out and meet with the customers and dealers who sold the electric motors. He enthusiastically explained to customers the advantages of the motors, and he listened carefully to what the customers and dealers wanted. He then communicated this information back to his colleagues in Engineering to help them focus on the parameters of the product that were important to the customer. Chris turned out to be an effective "leader from the middle." The vice president of Marketing let David Frank know that in several years, with the appropriate development, Chris could be a potential vice president of Marketing.

Building the Capability of Middle Managers

With the opening of markets outside the United States, it was clear that, both for new channels of distribution and to capitalize on the resources and skills available throughout the world, there were going to have to be better and more extensive linkages with companies outside the United States. EMI was going to have to engage in strategic alliances with companies in Europe as well as in the Far East in order to increase its marketshare growth outside the country. EMI was not going to be as competitive, either in price or features, unless it was able to leverage its current operations with resources from companies around the world. They saw some of their more forward-thinking competitors already making overtures to other companies to form alliances. One such alliance by a competitor was with a ceramics company to explore the development and application of ceramic materials in electronic motors. Middle managers were seen as the keys to executing the new kinds of relationships possible in external alliances. Top management was simply too busy to carry forward every possible alliance. In the new competitive, global environment that EMI had to operate, new vehicles to broaden the horizons of the middle managers were essential to prepare them for working effectively across organizations, cultures, and continents.

The direct boss of each middle manager was charged with sitting down with him and identifying the training needs for him to develop to be an effective general manager, if he was so inclined. Within three months the development needs for the majority of the middle managers were documented. These training needs, which were being coordinated by the Training Department, were then used for the selection of the internal and external programs that EMI should offer. Part of the recommendation was that greater emphasis be put on external training programs. It was felt that sending middle managers to programs outside the company, where they were exposed to middle managers from other companies and from other countries, would result in greater benefits to EMI. A major part of the broadening process could be accomplished by having EMI middle managers interact with fellow students who came from outside their industry and from outside the United States.

Holding Managers Accountable

The task force understood that people focus their attention on those things that are measured and rewarded. If what is measured and rewarded did not support the broadening role of middle managers, the recommendations would not take hold. The task force found that the appraisal process used for promotions, raises, and bonuses did not recognize the importance of working and integrating effectively across the organization. It was very much of a top-down process within each function. The boss set objectives and then evaluated his employee against those objectives a year later. This process did not recognize or allow for objectives across functional boundaries or get the input from people outside the middle-managers' unit. This was changed by altering the criteria for appraising managers. It started with David Frank's appraisal of the vice presidents. The task force recommended that David tell the vice presidents that he would evaluate them, and he would ask for the input of the other vice presidents on how well they worked together. This evaluation was going to be a factor in the determination of their raises and bonuses. Another factor to be used in the appraisal process was the openness of managers to moving people in and out of their organization. This assessment would be based on a manager's support of moving a good person out of his organization and his readiness to accept a person from another organization that he would have to train in order to do a job that others were already trained to do. Managers were also to be appraised on how well they performed in supporting the newly formed teams, specifically the ease with which they shared information with the interdepartmental teams and the ease with which they delegated to the teams the responsibility for decisions that previously they had made.

The final recommendation on rewards and appraisals was that promotion criteria should explicitly reflect emphasis on horizontal performance. People considered for promotion would be evaluated on how effectively they worked with peers in other parts of the organization and the initiative they showed in providing help and information to peers outside their functional unit.

These recommendations were accepted by the Executive Committee. They realized that in order to change their behavior and the behavior of the people in the organization, the reward system was going to have to recognize and reward the new kinds of behavior. But all this required new skills for the EMI managers—skills of team building, communication, using influence not authority—and a different view of their roles.

Developing New Skills in a
Balanced Organization

The orientation of most of the managers was that the organization operated in a vertical fashion. Direction came from the top, middle managers translated that direction to their subordinates, and the subordinates implemented it through operations. It was very clear that for horizontal and vertical dimensions to operate simultaneously, a new framework would be needed to create a balanced organizational structure. This framework would require that managers adopt a new view of their job, of how they manage, and of what they expect from their subordinates. They would have to become more comfortable delegating responsibility, working together with colleagues from different functional units, managing and being part of teams. Also, they would have to find a new source of power from which to carry out their responsibilities. No longer could they rely predominantly on their authority by virtue of their position in the hierarchy. They were going to have to base more of their ability to get things done on being able to work collaboratively as part of a problem-solving team of equals.

To help develop these new skills and attitudes, a five-day training program was developed that brought in cases and experts from the outside and utilized internal trainers as well. The training program was entitled "Managing Change," because its focus was on the external changes that the company was experiencing and how the company needed to adapt. It began with a discussion of strategy and what was required by the organization to effectively implement this strategy in the long term. It then covered the new and different kinds of people skills and management styles that were necessary. Cases based on the success and failure of individual managers within the company were discussed in order to better understand what the new behaviors were like in practice. Half-day sessions covered topics such as: problem solving, managing teams, and effective listening. The program was piloted with the Executive Committee and, after minor revisions, was offered to all managers.

The last session of the program was an identification of anything else that needed to be done in order to build a more effective horizontal organization. Participants in the program were organized into teams on the last day. They were asked to answer two questions:

1. What are the barriers to EMI's transitioning to a more effective horizontal organization?

2. What actions did the team recommend to overcome these barriers?

The trainers pulled together the responses after each program and sent them to the Executive Committee. The feedback provided by these answers was a way for EMI senior managers to monitor and adjust as EMI went through its transition to a more horizontal organization with greater leadership from the middle managers. These recommendations were carefully reviewed and implemented where appropriate. The participants from each program received feedback from the Executive Committee on their recommendations.

Other Actions to Strengthen the Horizontal Dimension

To further strengthen the horizontal linkages across functional units, several other actions were taken. One was to establish rewards for teams that worked together effectively. Up to now the reward system had been designed to recognize and reward only individual performance. The reward system was modified so that a pool of funds was available for teams. The bonuses would be given to teams based on three criteria: the achievement of the team's objective, the effectiveness and degree of teamwork within the team, and the amount of initiative and stretch the team used in solving the problem or dealing with the issue in front of it. The bonus for the team was to be decided by the Executive Committee or their delegate.

A second action to strengthen the horizontal dimension was to improve the rotation program. The rotation program up to then had been operating infrequently and informally at best. It needed to be more clearly structured and more carefully reviewed by the Executive Committee. The program was reoriented to concentrate more on middle managers. A minimum transfer would be one year into a different functional unit. The rotation needed to start early in a manager's career, often after his first promotion into middle management. Furthermore, for a rotation program to work, it needed to be integrated into the overall career plan or "road map" for the individual employee. The road map would identify when the rotation assignment would end and, if possible, what assignment would follow directly thereafter. If the next assignment could not be specified, at least the general direction of the move after that (e.g., into product management or a plant job) and plans for subsequent development were to be specified.

The vice president of each unit was asked to meet every two months with people who were on rotational assignment to their units. The vice presidents found they got useful feedback on their operations and on how well the new assignments were working out. This was an opportunity to monitor and adjust the rotation program within each unit to see that it was optimally beneficial for everyone involved.

A third action was to broaden the use of business teams beyond the three issues mentioned earlier as critical success factors. The task force recommended that the Executive Committee periodically establish two or three business teams that would focus on issues the Executive Committee identified as especially important. The teams would be changed to come up with recommendations. The issues identified for the next wave of business teams were:

- The redesign and implementation of new performance appraisals for individual and team performance;

- The design, development, and implementation of the five-day training program; and

- The examination of the flow of information to see how the computer system could be modified to make it easier to network across functional units.

Note that these issues focus on the management processes and systems of the organization, as described in Chap. 6.

The Executive Committee selected the team members and a leader. Each team was given no more than three months to examine its problem and come back to the Executive Committee with a final report, including an action plan. These reports were to be reviewed within three weeks by the Executive Committee and then given a go-ahead for implementation. The teams were kept together to implement the approved recommendations. After the conclusion of implementation, the monitoring of the implementation and the checking of progress became part of the permanent organization. The business team disbanded.

About every six months the Executive Committee identified two to three new areas for business teams to explore. The organization soon realized the benefits of bringing people together to solve problems and broaden their internal network of contacts. Barriers between units dropped as middle managers began to better understand the goals and operations of other units, and horizontal communication across units increased as middle managers got to know whom to call in other units. A subsidiary benefit for the Executive Committee was the opportunity to see talented middle managers who might not otherwise have been visible to them.

Required Changes in Management Behavior

It was clear that the model for the new behavior was going to have to come from the Executive Committee. David Frank initiated the definition of this new model by taking the Executive Committee offsite for two days to define what they needed to focus on as a team; that is, *what kinds* of questions, decisions, issues, and actions they could better decide as a team (e.g., corporate strategy) and *how* they were going to decide these issues. They also identified what decisions they did not have to make as a team and who had the responsibility to make these decisions (e.g., the amount of funding for new ceramic parts development was R&D's decision).

Next they identified the barriers to being more effective as a team, such as the lower priority they gave communication from outside their functional areas, the absence of a good understanding of the problems and constraints outside their own functional areas, extending even to a lack of knowledge of the goals of the other vice presidents. With the identification of each of these issues, the group developed action plans to overcome them. In most cases the actions were fairly obvious and straightforward, such as the sharing of goals, the participation of members from one vice president's staff in the staff meeting of another vice president, and so on. It was also decided that while David Frank was to be the primary champion for the change, the Executive Committee itself had to take ownership of the change throughout the organization. It was the entire Executive Committee that needed to champion and support the shift from the vertical to the horizontal organization. Each of them needed to be monitoring their subordinates on how well they were assisting people in other functional units, transferring information and ideas to other functional units, as well as initiating assistance, information, and information flow. All were expected to invite key people from other functions to participate in staff meetings and to get input on agendas and plans from colleagues in other functional units. They also recognized the need for each member of the Executive Committee to talk about the importance of this change, that is, to champion it through deeds and words.

Another aspect of bringing about this change was the importance of identifying the new style of management that would be necessary for the more effective managing of a horizontal organization. The Executive Committee identified the kinds of behavior that each member would have to engage in to move leadership to the middle managers and facilitate horizontal communication. These were most often the enabling behaviors described in Chap. 6. Other behaviors that would foster this change were initiative in providing information to other functional units and meeting management skills.

As part of this activity, all members of the Executive Committee got feedback from outside the Committee about their own performance of the enabling behaviors. The data were gathered from peers, subordinates, and superiors through interviews and questionnaires. In a two-day workshop the Executive Committee members analyzed this feedback and developed plans to modify their behaviors as appropriate. The Executive Committee met every six months thereafter for an evening, starting with dinner, in order to discuss how well they thought the transition was going and to continue the feedback process. These meetings helped build the teamwork across functions at the top level, which also served as a model for the middle managers.

Summary of EMI Actions

This section recaps the major actions and subordinate actions that EMI took to meet the demands of the New Competitive Reality and to turn around its performance.

1. EMI formed cross-functional teams of middle managers to identify major business challenges and to develop recommendations. Three major challenges were:
   - Introduction of manufacturing technology,
   - Communication between Engineering-Manufacturing and between Engineering-Marketing, and
   - Building middle-management capability.

2. Actions taken to improve communication between Engineering and Manufacturing:
   Step 1. Relocation of engineers to plants.
   Step 2. Formation of teams by product or operation.
   Step 3. One manager in charge of engineering/manufacturing team.

3. Actions taken to improve communication between Engineering and Marketing:
   Step 1. Rotation of engineers to Marketing.
   Step 2. Formation of product teams.

4. Actions taken to build middle-management capability:
   Step 1. Identification of development needs of middle managers that would enable them to become general managers.
   Step 2. Change in performance-appraisal criteria to emphasize:
   Teamwork,
   Sharing and rotating people, and
   Assisting peers.
   Step 3. Design and delivery of five-day "Managing Change" workshop.

5. Actions taken to strengthen the horizontal dimension:

Step 1. Bonus money set aside for teams.
Step 2. Improvements in the rotation program.
Step 3. Broader, continuous use of business teams.

6. Changes made by top management:
Step 1. Redefined how they were to operate together.
Step 2. Identified barriers to operating together and actions to reduce them.
Step 3. Examined own management style and developed plans for appropriate change.
Step 4. Reviewed progress as a team every six months.

To the Reader: In the Epilogue we return to EMI, two years from this point, to assess the results of these activities.

Who Said Leading from the Middle Would Be Easy?

The EMI example makes it clear that what we are asking for is no small change. This is not a minor tweak of the organization. It is nothing less than taking our conventional view of leadership and placing it at the middle-manager level. It is heresy according to all the principles, values, and beliefs of the traditional pyramidal structure. We believe that middle managers should not be governed by objectives set by their bosses. They should, of course, listen to what senior managers think, see, and say. But it is the middle managers who should be setting their own objectives.

If senior managers aren't effectively enabling middle managers to assert leadership, then they should be helped to learn to do so. To achieve this improvement in senior-manager performance requires that middle managers evaluate certain aspects of the performance of senior managers as an expected routine of the performance-evaluation process.

Middle managers are in a good position to take responsibility for initiative and decision making. Middle managers are closer to the customers, the technology, and the operations than are senior managers. But when middle managers do not have the information or resources they need, it is senior managers' responsibility to help them get what they need.

It is probably clear from this approach that the job of the senior manager has been transformed in this process. He or she is both "master" and "servant" for middle managers—a *master* in the sense of providing the direction, information, coaching, and encouragement—a *servant* in the sense of providing the resource help and support the middle manager requests and needs. This is not an easy job for the senior manager. Nor is it easy for the middle manager to make this transition. Some of the changes and the barriers to change for middle managers are described in the next chapter.

While the effort is difficult, the results—if the effort is maintained—are worth it. Both senior- and middle-level managers grow tremendously and feel much more satisfied about their work and lives.

Specific Ideas for Discarding Peter's Principle

1. At least monthly, inform everyone of the organization's and unit's performances. Be candid with the good and bad news.
2. For every problem ask for a one- or two-page analysis that consists of:
   a. A statement of the problem,
   b. An analysis of causes, and
   c. Recommended actions, indicating the person responsible and a schedule.
3. Look at the role of your staff groups. Are they "second-guessers" or facilitators of action? If they are not facilitators, change their roles, eliminate the group, or change the staff or structure.
4. Publicly recognize people who have taken risks—whether they succeeded or failed. Acknowledge the risk and the courage it took to take the risk.
5. Examine your performance-appraisal system and goal-setting process. Make sure they recognize "'people development" as an essential part of every manager's job.

Endnotes

1. *Intrapreneuring*, by Gifford Pinchot III (New York: Harper & Row, 1985) does a thorough job of discussing the potential and roadblocks to employees embarked on change.
2. Post-It™ Brand Notes are a trademark of 3M.
3. The 3M example of Post-It™ Notes is well known. However, there are literally thousands of such examples throughout U.S. corporations; the people behind these risks are unsung heroes.
4. For the reader interested in a broader discussion of these beliefs and attitudes and their impact on performance see *Directing Strategy The Keys to High Performance*, Englewood Cliffs, NJ: Prentice-Hall, 1992. The thinking of the authors, Lloyd Baird and Alan Frohman, is the basis for this chapter.

8
Taking Charge in the Middle

In the last chapter, we addressed the changes senior managers would have to make to develop and support leadership from middle managers. In this chapter we turn to the middle managers themselves. Middle managers, too, must adopt a different view of their roles and responsibilities if they are to take charge. This role is a marked change from the traditional view of a middle manager as a coordinator, translator, and go-between.[1]

The traditional view was appropriate for the organization of the 1960s, with a more stable environment, centralization, and divisionalization based on function. As noted in the earlier chapters, this situation is far from true today.

Middle Managers Step Up to Their New Role

Becoming Initiators, Not Just Go-Betweens

For organizations to succeed today, middle managers must view themselves less as go-betweens and more as initiators. Even the word *middle* in front of manager has the wrong connotation. It reinforces the hierarchy and sandwiching between levels. The term *middle* defines a position between two other positions, one higher, the other lower. But, alas, for now we will continue to use the term since most people understand what it means.

In most companies, middle managers have clung to their view of their jobs as requiring a high degree of specialization. This provides some feeling of security. Consider all the years required to be a specialist. The depth of expertise compiled over the years of specialization becomes the main source of added value and job security.

However, that has not only provided a false sense of security to middle managers, it has also been dysfunctional in its incompleteness. It suggests that success comes from depth, not breadth, and from narrow analysis rather than broad problem solving. It suggests that the middle manager is an analyst based on a special set of talents rather than a leader based on a broader set of problem-solving skills.

Here are two illustrations drawn from our experience that represent the contrast between these two perceptions:

The Initiator. Steve Walker, a project leader in R&D had just found out that the work his group had done on a proposal for a new tank guidance system was unsuccessful. Another firm had won the contract. He was convinced, however, that there were other markets for the guidance system. No one else seemed to agree. His boss wanted him to work on the next proposal. The marketing staff saw no use for the ideas in other markets.

Rather than take no for an answer, Steve began calling on potential users of the new guidance technology himself. He got his boss to at least not stop him, although his boss did not encourage him. He did not work with the marketing staff formally, but he did keep several colleagues in Marketing informed of his activities and solicited their advice. After numerous sales calls he found a company interested in sponsoring further development of the new guidance system. Steve felt vindicated in his view of the product's potential.

The Noninitiator. John Ganger, a chemist in R&D, came up with a startling new concept for removing stains from clothes. His boss suggested he write up the approach in a project proposal and submit it for funding in the budget for the next fiscal year. John did that. It was not funded because the technology was seen as having too small a chance to work. John and his fellow chemists in the lab thought differently but simply left it as "another example of their management being unwilling to take any risks."

In her writings, Rosabeth Moss Kanter has described three phases of accomplishment for a project.[2]

1. *Project definition:* Acquisition and application of information to shape a manageable, salable project.

2. *Coalition building:* Development of a network of backers who agree to provide resources and support.

3. *Action:* Application of the resources, information and support to the project and mobilization of an action team.

Steve Walker worked his way through each of these phases. His coalition was an informal one designed to avoid being blocked, which was all that he needed. Steve abandoned the rule of the hierarchy in favor of initiative taking to garner support from an ad hoc coalition. John rested comfortably on the principle of hierarchical authority and his aversion to risk taking.

Overcoming Organizational Barriers to Leadership

To get middle managers to act more like Steve and less like John will require radical change in the organization. There are numerous systems and practices in the typical organization that work against middle manager's taking the initiative. For example:

- Job descriptions, which define the limits of authority and responsibility. They usually state clearly to whom the person reports so as to reinforce the position *in the hierarchy.*

- Salary scales and job classifications, which give a strong sense of a person's place in the hierarchy and are the main point of reference in the reward system.

- Management by objectives usually refers to a process in which the boss determines the employee's objectives and evaluates progress against them. It is often a process of "management by the boss's objectives."

- Performance appraisals, like MBO, which are typically administered through the hierarchy with the immediate supervisor conducting the appraisal and the boss one level up signing the appraisal.

These types of systems and practices all need to be examined in light of their impact on middle-management initiative. As described in the last chapter, EMI focused considerable time and energy on examining and revising these systems in order to get more leadership from middle managers.

Accepting the Challenge

It is comfortable for middle managers to rely on job descriptions, policies and procedures, multiple levels of review and approvals. John Ganger did. It provides security and structure and reduces frustration. It provides a world that is organized, disciplined, and (more or less) certain. The hierarchy rules behavior. Problems are handled through policy and procedure. The bureaucracy provides a safety net of what is appropriate behavior and specifies how to handle what falls outside the net.

For this to change requires that senior managers do more than just push initiative taking and decision making down to the middle managers. It requires, in addition, that middle managers accept the challenge of taking the initiative. The answers we heard in a survey of 178 employees in a Fortune 500 company exemplify the attitudes that must change. This survey's objective was to better understand the current decision-making process in the corporation. Here is what some of the middle managers said:

> We don't make decisions because we don't know the boundaries of our jobs—I'm afraid of stepping on someone's toes.

> Middle managers aren't making decisions because of fear—they must have their roles defined and expectations set.

> I don't have the time to get all the data to make the decision. It has to be delegated up.

> My boss should delegate decisions that fit my capabilities. He does not know what they are.

All these quotes are from middle managers who aren't accepting the challenge. They are asking to be led down a clearly marked path. No such path exists in the complex, diverse environment of corporations attempting to adapt to the New Competitive Reality.

The question of placing blame or finding fault isn't the point here; nonetheless, we want to emphasize that it isn't the fault of middle managers that we hear these excuses. Many factors explain these attitudes. One of them, noted in Part 2, is that middle managers do not get sufficient information. This was evident in the company from which the previous quotes came as well. The 178 employees interviewed included middle managers (levels 6, 7, 8), those just below (level 5), and above (level 9). We found that employees in level 5 and those in level 9 and above were much more likely to receive the information they needed to make decisions on their job than were the middle managers. In fact, the lack of necessary information was more severely felt at the middle manager level than anywhere else in the firm.[3]

Controlling Emotional Barriers to Taking Charge

Other factors explaining why it is difficult for middle managers to accept the challenge were described by a middle manager at another U.S. corporation. She was discussing, in retrospect, a plan that she regretted having not questioned—a course of action that later resulted in catastrophe. Her insight and sensitivity are not commonplace.

> I regret that I did not question the plan before I moved. I can see now that a momentum was built up; I did not feel I could stop to think things through. We have a philosophy of pushing ever forward. To stop to question almost borders on disloyalty.
>
> We have a naive perspective, which is that if I try to make it work, it will somehow work even though I feel uneasy about what has happened. Some things will not work, but it is hard for me to call "stop" when there are so many factors I do not control. You must know when to end the investment and call everyone's attention to what is happening. In my job as a middle manager, what is my responsibility to try to make something work versus my obligation to raise doubts?

What did she risk by questioning the plan? She was concerned about her own feelings of disloyalty, about being accused of not being part of the team, about being chastised for questioning the ability of the group to pull it off, and about interfering with a momentum toward an important goal. These are very powerful forces. Combine these forces with vertical systems and procedures as well as an absence of information. Is it any wonder we do not see more leadership from the middle?

We describe these barriers not to deter middle managers from taking leadership. On the contrary, we want them to be aware of the magnitude of the challenge they face so as to better prepare themselves. We believe better preparation will lead to greater success and then to more frequent leadership initiatives. Our point is that the initiative must come from the middle managers, and it will never be easy to take it—only more or less difficult.

Taking Responsibility vs. Waiting for Delegation

Nor should middle managers expect delegation to occur naturally. Delegation is an *unnatural* act. Many managers feel that to delegate means to risk losing control, to err, and possibly to fail. To some extent this is correct, and so it is easy to understand why so many managers are reluctant to delegate. Delegation to individuals unprepared for the responsibility, unaware of the various courses of action, and unfamiliar with the consequences and costs of alternatives is, of course, foolish. Middle managers must demonstrate their readiness to take on additional responsibility by clearly assessing the situation and taking the responsibility for action.

Leadership is taken, not given.

Preparing to Lead: A Guide for Prudent Managers

Assess What Is Going On

Before taking on leadership from the middle, prudent middle managers will assess what is happening. There are many factors that bear on what the problem is and how to go about dealing with it. Going through the basic problem-solving steps can help develop a sound course of action.

- The goals of the situation and the criteria for selecting a course of action must be clear.

- The problem itself must be clearly defined, with symptoms and causes separated.

- A number of alternative courses of action should be generated, not just the first acceptable option.

- The various courses of action should be carefully and objectively weighed against the goals and criteria.

- An action plan should be developed, including how support for the plan will be gained, how the plan should be communicated, who should do what action according to what time schedule.

- Results should be checked periodically.

Mary Wilson, a middle manager, faced a situation of falling profits. The company had always assumed it could get more business by lowering its prices. It sold analytical testing services in a competitive market. Mary decided to assess the situation through customer surveys and focus groups. She found that customers were making their purchase decisions based, first, on quality and, second, on the experience of the scientist doing the work. Price was a distant fifth factor on the list. As a result, she began a campaign to gain support for shifting the strategy from cost competitiveness to raising the quality of the output and hiring experienced personnel. Her suggestions were implemented. She hit the nail on the head, and profits as well as sales increased sharply to record levels over the next year.

Middle managers also need to be astute with respect to what their bosses want. As noted by Gabarro and Kotter,[4] they should ask themselves:

- What does the boss want?
- Are his goals aligned with those of the organization? With mine?
- What are my goals? Are they aligned with those of the organization?
- What is my boss's style; that is, what behaviors does he tend to use more, less?
- What is my style? Is it compatible with my boss's?

Bill Williams, a middle manager, realized that the frequent one-on-one meetings he had with his previous boss wouldn't be held with his new boss. The new boss's style was to meet once a month with his fairly large staff. The rest of the time his schedule was filled by people who needed him to solve a problem or make a decision. Once Bill realized this, he no longer wondered why his boss did not set up regular meetings with him and was not responsive to his efforts to do so. His boss's style, whether good or bad, was not to work one on one.

While Bill could not change his boss's behavior, at least some of the tension Bill felt was removed. Bill came to understand that his new boss was encouraging him to be independent, to assume responsibility on his own. When a problem arose, he would use his boss if he had to, otherwise he was on his own.

Sue, a middle manager at a drug company, observed that even though her boss would never actively support a new initiative, he would never actually stop one. Consequently, she kept her boss informed of new-product developments, but she never asked for formal approval. She used her own budget and network of peers from other functions to get the additional information and resources she needed. Finally, when development had gone far enough to demonstrate technical and commercial feasibility, Sue brought it out for formal review and approval. Her boss reacted very positively to this approach.

Accept the Responsibility

For middle managers to take the initiative, they must accept that their responsibility will often exceed their authority. It is the responsibility of middle managers to ask questions, gather and assess information, formulate actions, and implement them based on what they feel should be done. They must often go *beyond* the formal limits of power and authority set forth in their job description.

This requires developing the courage and strength to go beyond what is formally sanctioned. It will not be easy. It requires tough mental and emotional discipline. To lead requires more strength than to follow. To question requires more strength than to simply obey orders.

Gary Burke is a plant manager for a major U.S. company. In 1975 he felt strongly that the traditional assembly-line mode of production was going to be too inefficient to be competitive within a decade. While some may have agreed with him, there was no one who wanted to deal with the problems of trying to establish a different type of production process in the plant. Such a change would upset a current, satisfactory mode of operating; risk subpar production; invite labor problems; and divert time and energy from ongoing operations. The other plant managers argued that it was not their responsibility to push for the analysis, testing, and piloting of new production methods. Gary felt otherwise. He felt he was responsible not only for day-to-day operations but also for the competitiveness of his plant in the future. He accepted this responsibility.

Gary began with visits to the plants of other companies that were using new production methods. He involved his people, both labor and management, in investigating new technologies. A team was put together to make a proposal for a phased-in set of changes that would, over three years, reshape the production process.

Selling the proposal was not easy. Many barriers stood in his way: obtaining capital, demonstrating a satisfactory rate of return, assessing products that were acceptable to the marketplace, and so on. Gary anticipated dealing with questions as part of his job and involved a wide range of people in gathering data. He then solicited support based on their findings. He put together a persuasive case. The risk was high in undertaking the new methods, but he designed an implementation process that would be done in phases, in order to reduce the risk. The project could be stopped at the end of each phase if analysis showed it made no sense to proceed.

Gary accepted responsibility across the board. He felt responsible for ensuring the competitiveness of his plant; he took the initiative to assess if there were better ways to do things and to study how they might be applied internally. He understood that it was necessary to marshall support for justifiable proposals if they were to actually be implemented. He worked to sell his proposals and to implement them once they were approved. At any point along the way he could have said "This is not my job" and stopped. It would have been easier and safer.

Gary, however, saw his job as creating change and challenging the status quo. In Kanter's term he was an "innovator"; that is, he went beyond the limiting parameters of his job description. He carried out the three phases of accomplishment that Kanter identifies: project definition, coalition building, and action.

Don't Be Deterred by the Prospect of Failure

It has been said we fear failure more than we covet success. Perhaps this is true. Human behavior is governed by attempts to avoid failure, and to avoid failure we play it safe. Make the decision in a way that you know the boss would approve. It may not be the best solution, but it is one that is safe. How many times have we seen a proposal rejected because the safest route was to not take a chance by trying something new? The expression, "If it isn't broken, don't fix it," justifies not rocking the boat.

Today, however, the phrase "continuous improvement" captures a different attitude—that to be competitive we must constantly try to do better. For this mindset to take hold requires that we accept that some things we try may not work out well. We are more vulnerable to failure.

Success and failure are strong words. If the middle manager sees his efforts as either succeeding or failing, then making decisions and taking actions become momentous undertakings. A different attitude is one of constant learning through trial and error. Improvements will not be the outcome of every attempt to change. In some cases, the effort will fall short; the learning will be the accomplishment.

At 3M, managers are expected to take risks, to try something new. They pride themselves on this culture of innovation. To support this culture, there are ample opportunities for managers initiating their own projects to seek out funds from a variety of sources. Any manager dissatisfied with the support he is able to gather in his present department is free to seek support and funding elsewhere. Managers can recruit their own teams and can go after an idea regardless of its size—no idea is too large or too small. If an idea doesn't work, the innovating middle managers are welcomed back into jobs equivalent to those they left.

Scott Marsh is an example of an initiative-taking manager. He developed a new type of aspirin that turned out not to pass initial tests for the adult market. He reacted to the disappointment by deciding to find out what else it could be used for. Other applications might require satisfying different criteria.

He took his idea of looking for new markets to the marketing people who asked the traditional customers the traditional questions and got traditional answers. No one wanted it.

Scott did not give up. He went out on the road and visited numerous pharmacists, hospitals, and doctors. At each step he described the aspirin and asked whether it would do anything that was useful. By the end of the trip he found his answer: a pleasant-tasting, chewable aspirin for children. Based on this new target, he undertook further development and testing. The new aspirin is now one of the company's most profitable products. Scott succeeded because he risked what was necessary to push from an idea to a business reality.

Be Prepared to Fight the Status Quo

Scott Marsh's experience illustrates another relevant point... that it is unrealistic to think people will easily accept a new idea. A middle manager must be prepared to battle the protectors of the status quo that are found at every level of most corporations. Our history is littered with the conclusive judgments of experts regarding the value of new ideas. A few examples of what the "experts" said follow:

> Far as I can judge, I do not look upon any system of wireless telegraphy as a serious competitor with our cables.
> —*Western Telegraph Company*, 1907

> That is the biggest fool thing we have ever done... the atom bomb will never go off and I speak as an expert in explosives.
> —*Admiral Leahy to President Truman*, 1945

> If that fellow has any sense he'll keep those observations to himself.
> —*Partner in J.P. Morgan & Co. to Billy Durant,*
> *who went home and put together General Motors*, 1908

> I say technically, I don't think anyone in the world knows how to do such a thing (intercontinental ballistic missiles) and I feel confident that it will not be done for a very long time to come... I think we can leave it out of our thinking.
>
> —*Vannevar Bush*, 1945

This message needs to be heeded by the middle manager and the senior manager.

The senior manager needs to withhold judgment, take a risk, and give new ideas a chance. Most organizations are set up to prevent change; it is usually regarded as a threat to security, and even an invitation to catastrophe. Change upsets plans, goals, systems, and lives. Typically, seniority and avoidance of mistakes get the rewards rather than risk taking and initiative.

Middle managers must have the courage to do what they think is right, instead of what the myriad of people in the hierarchy tell them to do. We are not talking about insubordination or a lack of respect; we're talking about courage that comes from conviction and self-respect.

The diagram in Fig. 8.1 displays the connections we are discussing. We are not suggesting any causal relationship. We feel that all these elements are necessary for taking the initiative. We believe that self-respect is based on a person's life experience.

As we noted earlier, Hewlett Packard uses the phrase "meritorious defiance." It is inscribed on an award that is given "...for contempt and defiance above and beyond the call of engineering duty." This is an apt phrase for what we call the courage to take leadership from the middle. It recognizes the need to go outside or even to subvert the normal channels.

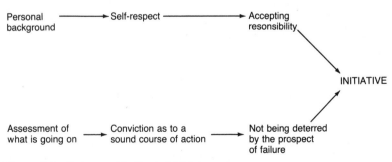

Figure 8.1. Factors contributing to initiative.

The Rocky Road of Innovation

Every innovative effort faces a rocky road. Innovation is a natural process of highs and lows, as we have seen in the previous cases. The process involves a series of setbacks and reversals as well as steps forward. The innovators are always vulnerable to failure.

Five typical stages can be identified in this process. During the first stage, *optimism*, gradually gives way to lessened enthusiasm and leads to the second stage, *struggle*. In many cases, unforeseen and unforeseeable problems arise and *disaster*, the third stage, strikes. Then, dogged perseverance leads to renewed and more realistic optimism, a preview for the fourth stage, *regeneration*. Finally, *compromises* are made, representing the fifth and final stage in this process. The original goals are altered, if need be, and the project approaches successful completion. Throughout this process of ups and downs, the middle manager must be patient and persevere since there will be setbacks all along the way. The road of innovation is hard, uncharted, and lonely.

Taking Charge

Executives in the United States have become experts at merging, purging, and leveraging. We need to do better at creating, innovating, and risk taking.

There are many reasons why there is an emphasis on merge, purge, and leverage. It is quick, action-oriented, visible, dramatic, and has a short-term focus. Results can be seen and can often be measured.

It will not, however, solve the problems brought about by the New Competitive Reality—problems of quality, innovation, speed, and the need for growth. These problems *cannot* be solved by senior managers; rather, senior managers can only make it either harder or easier for middle managers to solve them. It is up to the middle managers to display this leadership. They have, or can get, the information, technology, and resources to solve marketing, technology, manufacturing, and management problems. Middle managers may be correct when they blame senior managers for not creating the right conditions for leadership from the middle. However, only if middle managers are willing to accept the responsibility, to risk failure, and to display courage will their firm's competitiveness improve in the long run. The opportunities for change are within the reach of middle managers.

Specific Ideas for Taking Charge

1. Examine your job description; rewrite it if it does not recognize the role of the middle manager as an initiator. Do the same for your performance appraisal and management-development programs.

2. Be sure people are setting their own objectives based on whatever information they need to do it well.

3. Survey the people you work with to find out what information they need that they are not getting and get the information flowing.

4. Identify a problem or opportunity that deserves action and tackle it—now.

5. Take those good ideas you have been keeping to yourself and propose them to your boss. Use your colleagues as sounding boards.

6. List the three or four major problems facing your unit. Ask yourself what you would do if you were responsible for solving them. If it makes any kind of sense at all, take the initiative to start dealing with what you can.

7. Start with yourself: In what areas do you want to do better as a boss, peer, or employee. Pick the ones most important to you and develop an action plan. Start today.

Endnotes

1. See also "General Managers in the Middle," by Hugo Uyterhoven, *Harvard Business Review*, September-October, 1989, for a traditional view of the middle manager as go-between.

2. Rosabeth Moss Kanter, "The Middle Manager as Innovator," *Harvard Business Review*, July-August, 1982, Vol. 60, No. 4.

3. A number of surveys, while not trying to clarify differences between levels, have in fact significantly exposed them. See *Industry Week*, "Industry Practices," May 20, 1991, Vol. 240 No. 10, pp. 25–32.

4. For more on managing upward, see J. Gabarro and J. Kotter, "Managing Your Boss," *Harvard Business Review*, January-February, 1980. A well-done discussion of a relatively unexplored area.

Epilogue
EMI Two Years Later: The Payoff of Leading from the Middle

Refresher for the Reader

In 1988 EMI faced formidable competition and limited ability to respond. An analysis of the organization revealed inadequate initiative and horizontal linkages in the middle. Task forces were formed resulting in the following actions.

Summary of EMI Actions

1. EMI formed cross-functional teams of middle managers to identify major business challenges and to develop recommendations. Three major challenges were:
   - Introduction of manufacturing technology,
   - Communication between Engineering-Manufacturing and between Engineering-Marketing, and
   - Building middle-management capability.
2. Actions taken to improve communication between Engineering and Manufacturing:
   Step 1. Relocation of engineers to plants.
   Step 2. Formation of teams by product or operation.
   Step 3. One manager in charge of engineering/manufacturing team.
3. Actions taken to improve communication between Engineering and Marketing:
   Step 1. Rotation of engineers to Marketing.
   Step 2. Formation of product teams.

4. Actions taken to build middle-management capability:
   Step 1. Identification of development needs of middle managers that would enable them to become general managers.
   Step 2. Change in performance-appraisal criteria to emphasize:
   Teamwork,
   Sharing and rotating people, and
   Assisting peers.
   Step 3. Design and delivery of five-day "Managing Change" workshop.
5. Actions taken to strengthen the horizontal dimension:
   Step 1. Bonus money set aside for teams.
   Step 2. Improvements in the rotation program.
   Step 3. Broader, continuous use of business teams.
6. Changes made by top management:
   Step 1. Redefined how they were to operate together.
   Step 2. Identified barriers to operating together and actions to reduce them.
   Step 3. Examined own management style and developed plans for appropriate change.
   Step 4. Reviewed progress as a team every six months.

Two Years Later

Two years later, we talked with David Frank, EMI's president, about the results of the changes. His words best summarize what had occurred:

> My job is changing dramatically. No longer do I feel that the rest of the organization works for me; now I work for the organization. The original concept I had of my job as the sole leader was dysfunctional. Yes, we needed parts of it, but I was using too much of it. That view is based on the idea of control. I control the vice presidents, the vice presidents control their staffs, and so on down. No wonder the middle managers felt suffocated. They were walled off by layers of control. Now my job is one of unleashing, rather than controlling. I think of the organization as balanced—vertically and horizontally. This is consistent with thinking of a wave of energy as it moves from one part of the organization to another, linking the entire organization together, growing as the parts connect. In order to make sure I don't block this wave of energy, I watch it to see what I can do to remove the barriers to its progress and to provide resources for it to continue. I can't say my job is easier, but I can say that it's different and in many ways much more exciting.

Figures E.1 and E.2 present data regarding the productivity measures used by the organization. Figure E.3 compares product-development

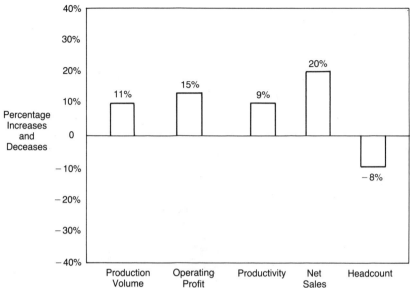

Figure E.1. EMI increases/decreases 1988–1990. In two years, without major benefits from new technology, EMI is seeing substantial payoff from the investment in its people. Sales increases were achieved against fierce competition in a stable market. Profit rose dramatically due to the increased productivity on a large fixed-asset base.

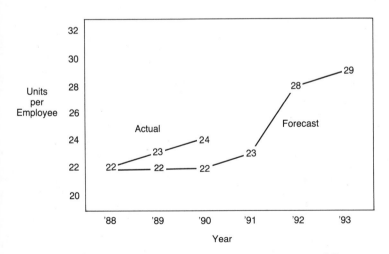

Figure E.2. Production per employee. Production per employee rose 9% in two years, significantly ahead of the forecast.

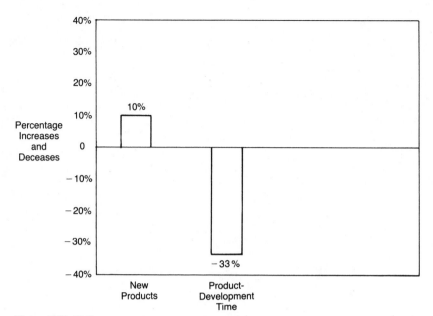

Figure E.3. EMI increases/decreases 1988–1990.

time and new product ideas with what had happened the preceding years. As you can see, the results are striking—in two years productivity had increased even beyond what was called for in the business plan; new-product development time was cut, and the number of new products introduced had increased.

EMI had tried to achieve ambitious goals before and fallen short. Now, in 24 months they had been able to dramatically improve things, and they anticipated that this trend would continue. Let us listen to the comments of the EMI middle managers who, two years later, felt like they were working in a revitalized organization.

> I knew something was bothering me. I had worked for EMI for 12 years and somehow felt suffocated. I enjoyed my work and worked hard, but I wasn't being fully utilized. Now, with the shift toward the balanced organization, it's clear to me what it was. I was working within overly constraining functional boundaries, goals, tasks, and information. With this new horizontal organization, these constraints have been removed. I feel like I can breath fresher air. This has been a major change and I'm very excited about it.

> It isn't easy managing horizontally as well as vertically. There are a lot of problems and barriers. But at least now I'm getting on with the job. At least

now I'm tackling the problems that are important to the organization and to the success of my work. Before, I was dealing with narrow political and operational problems.

I have grown more in the last year than in my entire career to this point with the organization. [He had been with EMI for over 20 years.] The exposure to the marketing organization [he is an engineer] has enabled me to see and understand things that I never thought about before.

EMI underwent a major change, a change it needed to go through in order to respond to the threats and opportunities in its environment. But these threats and opportunities are no different than the ones talked about in Chap. 1. Its problems, too, are no different than the problems documented in Chap. 3 in Salesco, Matco, and Techco where the lack of an effective horizontal organization produced performance deficits on the part of the employees as well as the organization. What EMI did was acknowledge these problems and put in place the many changes, starting with top management, that could address them. It was not easy to do this, because it required changes in organization, structure, and systems, as well as and most importantly, in individual behavior starting with the top managers. EMI continues to shift effectively to a balanced organization with the unleashing of leadership from middle managers, the effective use of teams, enhanced lateral communication, and the broadening and development of people beyond functional knowledge bases. It is a massive change that EMI has undergone, but it is one that has equipped the organization to deal with the New Competitive Reality.

Suggestions for Additional Readings

Careers

Baird, Lloyd and K. Kram, "Managing the Superior Subordinate Relationship," *Organizational Dynamics*, Spring, 1983. This article focuses on the impact of career stages on the dynamics of the relationship between bosses and their subordinates. It is one of the most popular reprints from *Organizational Dynamics*.

Bardwick, Judith M., *The Plateauing Trap*, AMACOM, New York, 1985. This book describes the changing environment facing middle managers and discusses the resulting impact on their careers and lives. Bradwick recommends a series of approaches for dealing with the personal impact of what we call "the gap in the middle."

Bridges, William, *Transitions: Making Sense of Life's Changes*, Addison Wesley, Reading, MA, 1980. Bridges presents a strategy for dealing with changes in our careers and personal lives. This is a very useful book for people facing major changes at midlife, as well as at other times in their lives.

Leadership and Empowerment

Beckhard, Richard and W. Pritchard, *The Essence of Change: The Art of Creating and Leading Fundamental Change in Organizations*, Jossey-Bass, San Francisco, 1992. Dick Beckhard's latest book, written with London-based consultant Wendy Pritchard, is a concise, practice-based, prescription of the type of change needed for survival in today's competitive world—a process the authors call fundamental change.

Bennis, Warren and B. Nanus, *Leaders: The Strategies for Taking Charge*, Harper & Row, New York, 1985. The dean of writers on leadership, Warren

Bennis stresses the role of a leader as creating and communicating a vision. Collaborating with Bert Nanus, he makes a persuasive case for empowerment.

Carlzon, Jan, *Moments of Truth,* Harper & Row (Perennial Library Edition), New York, 1989. Carlzon, the CEO of Scandinavian Airlines System, was the architect of the turnaround of SAS in the early 1980s. He describes visioning and empowering as the keys to the turnaround.

Kotter, John P., *A Force for Change: How Leadership Differs from Management,* Free Press, New York, 1990. One of the most effective writers on leadership, Kotter makes a clear distinction between the approach and practices of leaders in contrast to those of managers. Kotter suggests that the essence of leadership is managing change.

Kouzes, James and B. Posner, *The Leadership Challenge,* Jossey Bass, San Francisco, 1987. Based on extensive survey data, Kouzes and Posner have created a useful approach for people at all levels in organizations to develop their leadership potential. The authors hold strongly to the view that "leaders are made, not born."

Middle Management

Block, Peter, *The Empowered Manager: Positive Political Skills at Work,* Jossey-Bass, San Francisco, 1987. Peter Block describes how middle managers can overcome the negative politics in organizations that can prevent them from taking responsibility. In addition, Block discusses the changes that are required in relationships when the subordinate takes on greater responsibility.

Kanter, Rosabeth Moss, *The Change Masters,* Simon & Schuster, 1983. Rosabeth Kanter discusses how vital a climate for innovation is for organizational effectiveness. She outlines the strategies a middle manager should follow to become an innovator.

Kanter, Rosabeth Moss, *When Giants Learn to Dance: Mastering the Challenges of Strategy, Management and Careers in the 1990s,* Simon & Schuster, New York, 1989. Drawing on examples from her extensive consulting experience in major U.S. corporations, Kanter suggests a survival plan for middle managers in today's downsized, restructured world.

Pinchot, Gifford III, *Intrapreneuring,* Harper & Row, New York, 1985. Pinchot coined the term "intrapreneur" to describe the process of being entrepreneurial in large organizations. This is a very practical book full of lessons from a range of successful intrapreneurs.

Organizational Practices and Change

Baird, Lloyd S. and A. L. Frohman, *Directing Strategy: Keys to High Performing Organizations,* Prentice Hall, Englewood Cliffs, NJ, 1992. The authors, one a coauthor of this book, describe five key management practices that can bring out the best in people and organizations. They also indicate how to apply these practices in organizations.

Grove, Andrew S., *High Output Management,* Random House, New York, 1983. As a cofounder and President of Intel, Grove is a scientist and entrepreneur with many creative and thought-provoking ideas about managing people in a high-tech environment. As just one example, Grove makes a clear and concise argument why senior management should commit to creating and leading a meaningful performance appraisal process.

Handy, Charles, *The Age of Unreason,* Harvard Business School Press, Cambridge, MA, 1989. A well-known British teacher and management consultant, Handy outlines the types of changes in organizational design and structure needed to adapt to a rapidly changing external environment. In addition, he shows how these changes will affect people's careers in the future.

Kidder, Tracy, *The Soul of a New Machine,* Little Brown, Boston, 1981. Tracy Kidder won a well-deserved Pulitzer Prize for this book about the superhuman efforts of a team at Data General to develop a new computer. This book is a remarkable look at what motivates people—and teams—to do outstanding work under pressure.

Pascarella, Perry and M. Frohman, *The Purpose-Driven Organization,* Jossey-Bass, San Francisco, 1989. The authors describe the benefits of a clearly formulated and communicated organizational purpose. They give examples and present steps for developing and using purpose statements for all types of organizations. Their arguments are compelling.

Peters, Tom, *Thriving on Chaos,* Knopf, New York, 1987. This is a handbook for managing complex organizations facing constant change. For managers at every level, Peters prescribes a wide ranges of specific actions necessary for survival in today's chaotic environment.

Zuboff, S., *In the Age of the Smart Machine,* Basic Books, New York, 1988. Zuboff describes the current and likely future impact of computers and information systems on people, their organizations, and organizational practices.

Appendix:
Sample Questions from Strategy Implementation Survey

Note: In this appendix, we have omitted a number of individual questions from the Survey in order to make it more useful to the reader. Typically, a complete survey has more than 100 questions, including a number directly related to the specific organization.

GENERAL INSTRUCTIONS

This survey contains a number of questions and statements about the mission, objectives, structure, and other related issues. Most of the questions ask that you circle one of several numbers that appear on a scale next to the question; some ask that you fill in some information.

When making your choice from a scale, choose the one number that best matches your view or opinion about the question. For example, if you were to be asked how important the weather is to your selection of a vacation spot, and you feel that it is extremely important, you circle the number 7 "Extremely important" like this:

How important is the weather to your selection of a vacation spot?

1	2	3	4	5	6	7
Not at all important			Important			Extremely important

Please note that the scale descriptions are different for different questions in the survey. For example, one may ask how much you agree or disagree with a particular issue, while another question may ask how clear something is. *SO BE SURE TO READ THE ANSWER SCALE BEFORE CHOOSING YOUR RESPONSE.*

* * * * * * * * * * * * * *

PART I
DEMOGRAPHIC INFORMATION

The information contained in this section is needed to help us in the statistical analysis of the survey data. All of your responses are kept strictly confidential; individual responses will not be given to anyone within.

PART II
A. MISSION

These first questions are about the Mission. When answering, please keep in mind your experiences working at _____. Place a circle around the one number on the scale which most nearly represents your view.

1. What is our current competitive position in the U.S. market?

1	2	3	4	5	6	7
At a GREAT DISADVANTAGE			Neither Advantage nor Disadvantage			At a GREAT ADVANTAGE

2. Is the mission clear to you?

1	2	3	4	5	6	7
Not at all clear; I do NOT understand what the mission really is		Somewhat clear		Pretty clear		Very clear; I have a good understanding of what the mission really is

These next questions are about your personal reactions to the mission statement. They ask about your current views and whether they are changing.

3. How enthusiastic are you about supporting this mission?

1	2	3	4	5	6	7
I am NOT AT ALL enthusiastic		Somewhat enthusiastic		Pretty enthusiastic		I am extremely enthusiastic

4. How confident are you that _____ can achieve this mission?

1	2	3	4	5	6	7
I am NOT in any sense confident		Somewhat confident		Pretty confident		I am extremely confident

5. How much are you personally contributing to the success of this mission?

1	2	3	4	5	6	7
I am NOT contributing at all		I am contributing somewhat		I am contributing a good deal		I am making a very significant contribution

B. BUSINESS OBJECTIVES

For each of the following items, circle the number which best represents your view of:
(A) How well _____ is doing now
(B) Whether _____ is getting better at accomplishing each objective

1. *CUSTOMER SATISFACTION*: Improve Customer Satisfaction to be the industry leader.

A. How well is _____ doing now?

1	2	3	4	5	6	7	8
MUCH WORSE! Worsening everyday!			NO CHANGE			MUCH BETTER Improving everyday!	NO OPINION

2. *PEOPLE DEVELOPMENT*: Improve the quality, capability and promotability of _____ employees.

A. How well is _____ doing NOW?

1	2	3	4	5	6	7	8
TERRIBLE Could Not be worse!			SO-SO			FANTASTIC Could not be better!	NO OPINION

B. Is _____ getting better at this?

1	2	3	4	5	6	7	8
MUCH WORSE Worsening everyday!			NO CHANGE			MUCH BETTER Improving everyday!	NO OPINION

3. *INNOVATION/BUSINESS EFFECTIVENESS:* Improve _____ use of new "state-of-the-art" technology.

A. How well is _____ doing NOW?

1	2	3	4	5	6	7	8
TERRIBLE Could not be worse!			SO-SO			FANTASTIC Could not be better!	NO OPINION

B. Is _____ getting better at this?

1	2	3	4	5	6	7	8
MUCH WORSE Worsening everyday!			NO CHANGE			MUCH BETTER Improving everyday!	NO OPINION

PART III

This part of the survey deals with some specific issues/constraints involved with the Mission and Objectives.

COMMUNICATION/COOPERATION

The following questions ask you about the flow of communications from higher level management within _____ down to your level and from your level up to higher management. For each statement, indicate how much you AGREE or DISAGREE with it.

I. DOWNWARD FLOW

	Strongly Disagree	Disagree	Slightly Disagree	Neither Agree nor Disagree	Slightly Agree	Agree	Strongly Agree
1. Top management has made an effort to inform me about new mission and objectives..................	1	2	3	4	5	6	7

II. UPWARD FLOW

	Strongly Disagree	Disagree	Slightly Disagree	Neither Agree nor Disagree	Slightly Agree	Agree	Strongly Agree
1. I feel free to tell people higher up in ———— what I really think...........	1	2	3	4	5	6	7

> The following questions ask you to indicate the extent of communication and cooperation between different functional groups within ————.

III. CROSS-FUNCTIONAL INFORMATION

TO WHAT EXTENT ...

	Not At All			Somewhat			To A Great Extent
a. ...do you need information from other parts of.............	1	2	3	4	5	6	7
b. ...do you get the information you need from other parts of	1	2	3	4	5	6	7
c. ...do you need cooperation from other parts of	1	2	3	4	5	6	7
d. ...do you get the cooperation you need from other parts of	1	2	3	4	5	6	7

STRUCTURE

The following questions ask you about the internal structure of formal authority and information flow within _____. For each statement, indicate how much you AGREE or DISAGREE with it.

	Strongly Disagree	Disagree	Slightly Disagree	Neither Agree nor Disagree	Slightly Agree	Agree	Strongly Agree
1. Decisions get slowed down by red tape and bureaucracy in _____	1	2	3	4	5	6	7
2. In _____, it is not clear who has the formal authority to make a decision................	1	2	3	4	5	6	7

DELEGATION/DECISION MAKING

These next questions are about the level of formally delegated decision-making authority within and on your job. For each statement, indicate how much you AGREE or DISAGREE with it.

	Strongly Disagree	Disagree	Slightly Disagree	Neither Agree nor Disagree	Slightly Agree	Agree	Strongly Agree
1. Decisions are delegated to the lowest possible levels in _____	1	2	3	4	5	6	7
2. My supervisor gives me the freedom to make changes in the way I do my work...............	1	2	3	4	5	6	7

TEAM CONCEPT

The following items are concerned with team membership. Circle the number which most nearly represents your feelings.

I. MEMBERSHIP

TO WHAT EXTENT...

	Not At All			Somewhat			To A Great Extent
	1	2	3	4	5	6	7

a. ....do you feel a part of your business unit's team ....

> These next questions deal with relationships within your work unit and between your work unit and other units in
> _____.

II. MY WORK GROUP

	Strongly Disagree	Disagree	Slightly Disagree	Neither Agree nor Disagree	Slightly Agree	Agree	Strongly Agree
	1	2	3	4	5	6	7

a. People in my work unit work well as a team.................. 1 2 3 4 5 6 7

b. The goal of my work unit is to be the best at whatever we do 1 2 3 4 5 6 7

III. OTHER WORK GROUPS

	Strongly Disagree	Disagree	Slightly Disagree	Neither Agree nor Disagree	Slightly Agree	Agree	Strongly Agree
	1	2	3	4	5	6	7

a. Different units within _____ work together to reach a common goal 1 2 3 4 5 6 7

b. There is a lot of tension and rivalry between units within _____ 1 2 3 4 5 6 7

PEOPLE DEVELOPMENT

These questions are about rewards, e.g., promotions and pay increases. Circle the number which best represents your view on how they are handled.

	Strongly Disagree	Disagree	Slightly Disagree	Neither Agree nor Disagree	Slightly Agree	Agree	Strongly Agree
1. We have a promotion system in _____ that helps the best person to rise to the top..............	1	2	3	4	5	6	7
2. In _____, people are rewarded in proportion to their job performance..............	1	2	3	4	5	6	7
3. To get ahead in _____ it's more important to get along than it is to be a higher producer	1	2	3	4	5	6	7

These next questions concern your opportunities to develop your skills and abilities on the job. Circle the number which best represents your views.

TO WHAT EXTENT DO YOU GET …

	Not At All		Somewhat				To A Great Extent
4. ….the training opportunities you need to improve your current job performance?..............	1	2	3	4	5	6	7
5. ….the help from your supervisor that you need to improve your current job performance?..............	1	2	3	4	5	6	7
6. ….the developmental assignments you need to improve your current job performance?..............	1	2	3	4	5	6	7

The following items are concerned with the organizational culture or context in which the mission and objectives must be carried out.

SHORT-TERM/LONG-TERM

Here are some statements about the type, extent, and focus of planning which goes on in _____. Please indicate how much you AGREE or DISAGREE with each statement.

	Strongly Disagree	Disagree	Slightly Disagree	Neither Agree nor Disagree	Slightly Agree	Agree	Strongly Agree
1. Management does not plan ahead in _____	1	2	3	4	5	6	7
2. Our productivity sometimes suffers from a lack of organization and planning	1	2	3	4	5	6	7

MANAGERIAL PERSPECTIVE

These next items concern the ability of management and others within _____ to foresee and focus on issues beyond the immediate. Indicate how much you AGREE or DISAGREE with each statement.

	Strongly Disagree	Disagree	Slightly Disagree	Neither Agree nor Disagree	Slightly Agree	Agree	Strongly Agree
1. People here generally pay attention to their own functional area and don't worry about how they could help to succeed	1	2	3	4	5	6	7
2. My supervisor often "doesn't see the forest for the trees."	1	2	3	4	5	6	7

RISK TAKING

These statements are about risk taking and trying new things within _____. Circle the number which best represents your view.

	Strongly Disagree	Disagree	Slightly Disagree	Neither Agree nor Disagree	Slightly Agree	Agree	Strongly Agree
1. ____ management encourages people to take risks and try new things.	1	2	3	4	5	6	7
2. People who get a head in ____ are willing to stick their necks out and try new things.	1	2	3	4	5	6	7
3. My supervisor supports me when I take risks.	1	2	3	4	5	6	7

PROBLEM SOLVING

> The following statements deal with the way problems are handled within ____. Circle the number which best represents how much you AGREE or DISAGREE with each statement.

	Strongly Disagree	Disagree	Slightly Disagree	Neither Agree nor Disagree	Slightly Agree	Agree	Strongly Agree
1. ____ management works openly with people to solve problems when they arise	1	2	3	4	5	6	7
2. When problems arise in ____ people look for someone to blame	1	2	3	4	5	6	7
3. When problems arise in ____, people ignore them and wait for them to go away	1	2	3	4	5	6	7
4. In ____, we look for a "quick fix" rather than a long-term solution to problems	1	2	3	4	5	6	7

TOP-DOWN APPROACH

> These items concern management's approach to interacting with different levels within.

	Strongly Disagree	Disagree	Slightly Disagree	Neither Agree nor Disagree	Slightly Agree	Agree	Strongly Agree
1. Top management at ____ doesn't like to hear about problems or other negative issues.	1	2	3	4	5	6	7
2. Decisions are made in ____ without ever asking the people who have to live with them	1	2	3	4	5	6	7

ACTION ORIENTATION

These next items are about a management orientation to follow through from plans to actions and finally to end results. Please indicate how much you AGREE or DISAGREE with each as a description of managers.

	Strongly Disagree	Disagree	Slightly Disagree	Neither Agree nor Disagree	Slightly Agree	Agree	Strongly Agree
1. In ____ looking busy is more important than results	1	2	3	4	5	6	7
2. My supervisor is clearly concerned with accomplishing our unit's work objectives	1	2	3	4	5	6	7

PEOPLE ORIENTATION

These statements deal with the level of concern for people demonstrated by ____ management. Please circle the number which best represents your feelings.

	Strongly Disagree	Disagree	Slightly Disagree	Neither Agree nor Disagree	Slightly Agree	Agree	Strongly Agree
1. _____ management cares more about money and machines than people	1	2	3	4	5	6	7
2. Top management in _____ is genuinely interested in developing people	1	2	3	4	5	6	7
3. Top management believes that people are the most valuable asset	1	2	3	4	5	6	7

* * * * * * * * * * * * *

THIS COMPLETES THE SURVEY.

Thank you for completing this important part of the survey. Your answers will help.

This page gives you the opportunity to say, in your own words, what you think about the mission, objectives, and work environment. Please use the space below for that purpose and attach additional sheets, if necessary.

Do you have any comments on how we can improve this survey?

Once again, thank you for your cooperation. Please use the stamped envelope to return your completed survey. Thank you.

Index

About the Authors

Alan L. Frohman is president of Frohman Associates, Inc., a Lexington, Massachusetts international consulting firm specializing in strategic planning and change, organizational development, and technology management. He is also a regular contributor to professional business journals, a sought-after speaker on management topics, and the author of *Directing Strategy Keys to High Performance.*

Leonard W. Johnson is currently executive-in-residence at the Boston University School of Management, where he is teaching MBA courses in organizational behavior, leadership, managing conflict and change, and career development. He is also a senior consultant at Frohman Associates, Inc., where he is an expert on middle management issues.